Thinking Anthropologically

Thinking Anthropologically

A PRACTICAL GUIDE FOR STUDENTS

Third Edition

Philip Carl Salzman
McGill University

Patricia C. Rice
West Virginia University

Co-Editors

Prentice Hall
Boston   Columbus   Indianapolis   New York   San Francisco   Upper Saddle River   Amsterdam
Cape Town   Dubai   London   Madrid   Milan   Munich   Paris   Montreal   Toronto   Delhi
Mexico City   Sao Paulo   Sydney   Hong Kong   Seoul   Singapore   Taipei   Tokyo

Editor in Chief: Dickson Musslewhite
Publisher: Nancy Roberts
Editorial Assistants: Nart Varoqua and Kate Fernandes
Director of Marketing: Brandy Dawson
Senior Marketing Manager: Laura Lee Manley
Marketing Assistant: Pat Walsh
Production Manager: Fran Russello
Cover Manager: Jayne Conte
Cover Designer: Suzanne Behnke
Cover Image Credit: J. Terrance McCabe
Full-Service Project Management: Aparna Yellai, GGS Higher Education Resources, PMG
Printer/Binder: Courier Companies, Inc.
Text Font: New Baskerville

Library of Congress Cataloging-in-Publication Data
Thinking anthropologically : a practical guide for students / Philip Carl Salzman, Patricia C.
  Rice.—3rd ed.
    p. cm.
Includes bibliographical references and index.
ISBN-13: 978-0-205-79271-9
ISBN-10: 0-205-79271-5
1. Anthropology—Philosophy.   2. Anthropology—Methodology.   I. Salzman, Philip Carl.
  II. Rice, Patricia C.
GN33.T45 2011
301.01—dc22

                                                                              2010005195

                                                           10 9 8 7 6 5 4 3 2 1

Prentice Hall
is an imprint of

www.pearsonhighered.com
ISBN 10:   0-205-79271-5
ISBN 13: 978-0-205-79271-9

Contents

Introduction to the Third Edition

We, the editors and authors of *Thinking Anthropologically*, would like to thank the instructors who followed our advice and wrote us about what they (and their students) liked and did not like about the second edition. Several told us they thought a glossary would have been helpful as well as study questions or homework questions at the end of individual chapters. We are happy to again accommodate these items as well as a general index for the third edition. One instructor suggested we incorporate in-class activities for each chapter. Many in-class activities appear in a "how to do it" format in the *Strategies in Teaching Anthropology* series, published by Pearson.

We also introduce two new chapters for this edition: the first is on a topic we quite frankly previously overlooked in the second edition—thinking about sex/gender biologically, archaeologically, linguistically, and culturally. We are happy that Paloma Gay y Blasco joined us in writing that important chapter. Professional anthropologists think anthropologically when they begin to think about doing research in their particular area of expertise and realize how vital it is to define concepts and set up criteria. We feel students should begin to think anthropologically about how we go about doing research so they can better understand the nature of the anthropological paradigm. The second new chapter focuses on fieldwork, an important part of most anthropologists' lives; some start fieldwork as undergraduates but all begin by graduate school. In this case, because fieldwork is so personal to each subfield of anthropology, we asked four teaching anthropologists to discuss their particular subfield's field component.

We also want to thank the authors of the second edition who agreed to take advice and revise their original contributions. They believe, as we do, that for their maximum benefit, students can and should think anthropologically at the beginning of the term.

We'd like to acknowledge those individuals who reviewed this text: Jonathan S. Marion, California State University San Marcos, David R. Bush, Heidelberg College and Howard A. Doughty, Seneca College.

CHAPTER 1

Introduction to Thinking Anthropologically

Philip Carl Salzman
McGill University

Patricia C. Rice
West Virginia University

PART 1: FOR STUDENTS ONLY

When I (Salzman) was a freshman at Antioch College in Ohio, I took an introductory philosophy course. In preparing for each class, I usually read at least some of the assigned reading in the collection of selections from great philosophers. But when I got to class and the professor began talking about the assigned reading, I recognized nothing in what I had read from what he was saying. There seemed to be no overlap between what I understood from the text and what the professor was telling us it was about. I might as well have been reading *Dilbert*.

As you can imagine, this was a rather disconcerting experience. But in a way, it was inevitable. Why? Because I had no clue as to the frames of reference that philosophers used to situate their discussions. I did not know what philosophers thought were problems, how they intended to address them, or even what they thought would count as answers. In other words, I had no idea how to think philosophically.

When I (Rice) was an undergraduate up the road from Antioch College at Ohio State University, I took my first economics course and had an experience similar to my co-editor. What I read and what the instructor said, supposedly about the same material, were as different as night and day. The terminology was a kind of foreign language, but I could cope with that. What was frustrating and unnerving was the fact that I hadn't a clue as to how to think economically. This did improve during the term, but not until an hour before the final exam did it all become clear. At the time, I called it the "aha" syndrome, but I now know that only at the last minute was I beginning to think economically. If I had begun to think economically at the beginning instead of the end of the course, I am sure I would have been less frustrated and would have learned a good deal more. We hope this book will help you to avoid that kind of experience by learning how to think anthropologically early in your first anthropological adventure in the classroom.

Such frustrations occur in any new field that you study, whether physics, literature, history, or anthropology. When we begin to explore a new field, we enter our exploration at one time and place, a little like taking the first steps off a beach into a lake or sea. It is impossible for us to know all of the other points at which we might have stepped into the water, the overall shape of the water body, and how it affects the place into which we have stepped.

Your instructor, however knowledgeable and good at communicating, cannot talk about everything at once. He or she cannot tell you at the same time about specific ethnographic cases and about different kinds of societies, or about epistemological assumptions about how we learn things at the same time as about ethnographic **fieldwork** methods, or about general heuristic theories at the same time as about specific understandings of particular cultural patterns. He or she cannot tell you about Darwin's and Mendel's contributions to evolution at the same time he or she is discussing the details of *Australopithecus robustus*, much less the ecological context and why we think this population adapted to life on the savanna. You eventually need to know all of these things and how they influence one another, but you cannot learn all of it at once. Be patient; you will catch on.

Well, we have a bit more to offer than "be patient." The short chapters in this collection are clear explanations of the underlying frameworks assumed and used by anthropologists. What does your instructor mean by "theory"? You will find some answers to this in Chapter 4. When your instructor talks about studying culture, what does she or he mean? Chapter 2 will give you some clues to this question. Why do anthropologists disagree, and how can you learn about anthropology when anthropologists can't even agree among themselves? Chapter 7 discusses this issue. After you read these chapters, you will begin to *think anthropologically*. This will help you understand your instructor and the assigned readings better and will help you do better in the course.

The authors of each chapter are teaching anthropologists who, like your instructor, see students who are brand new to anthropology every term. Most teach introductory courses as well as advanced courses in their specialties. They all have their interests and biases and may not all agree that the theme of each chapter is the single most important aspect of anthropology. For example, some may be humanist anthropologists who believe descriptions of other cultures and attempts to find cultural meaning are the most important part of anthropology, whereas others may be scientists who attempt to explain particular aspects of what it is to be human. Some may feel ethics should be the focus of each topic, while others may limit ethics to professional audiences. Some feel very strongly that the importance and fun of anthropology lie in the interrelatedness of its parts—the past and the present, culture and biology—whereas others are perfectly happy teaching and researching only one subfield. Some feel very strongly that if we anthropologists do not apply our knowledge, we are giving up an opportunity to help others, whereas some feel that our main obligation is increasing knowledge. And this profile fits anthropologists in general, not just the authors of these chapters. We all think anthropologically, however, and believe that this thinking is at the heart of what we do and what we teach. We want to share this experience with you while we impart some knowledge about what it is to be human.

We believe that this book will help you understand anthropology, but perhaps future editions can be even more useful. We would like to ask you to help us improve this book for future students by telling your instructor whether you found it helpful, which chapters were most useful, which ones were least useful, and what other subjects you wish had been covered. Working together, we can help other students to *think anthropologically*.

PART 2: FOR INSTRUCTORS ONLY

Anthropology, like individual cultures, is a complex, interrelated system of meaning with different levels of understanding and multiple alternative interpretations. Addressing any particular ethnographic fact, heuristic theory, mode of analysis, fieldwork methodology, or epistemological presumption implies reference to other facts, theories, modes, methodologies, and presumptions and leads one up and down to different levels of understanding and to other interpretations. The same is true of **paleoanthropology**, with its additional element of attempting to find and evaluate evidence in the past without being able to see events as they occur, revisit data for verification, or even talk with people.

There is no ideal way to introduce anthropology to students. Wherever we start, we must fan out in all directions, reach up and down, make connections, and survey the landscape. Whatever we start with, we must end up someplace else. If we begin with the very general, we must proceed to the particular; if we begin with the particular, we must advance to the general. We can start with individual ethnographies but will eventually get to a discussion of religion, economy, and kinship; we can begin with religion and politics but end with hunters and cultivators. We can discuss Old World and New World pyramids in terms of architectural similarities but end up discussing differences of function; we can begin comparing primate femurs and end up with a discussion of different locomotor patterns and why hominid bipedalism evolved.

So wherever we begin, whatever we begin to teach our students about anthropology, there are 23 or 230 other places we are not teaching about that are implied in what we are saying or that are necessary to conceptualize it. Of course, we cannot speak about everything at once. We must start at one point and proceed around the great circle of anthropology. And our students must learn about one thing at a time, initially oblivious to its connections with all of the rest. This is inevitable and cannot be avoided.

However, to paraphrase John Dewey, this anthropological reality is not a problem because there is no solution to it. But this challenge is the raison d'être for *Thinking Anthropologically*. This readily available supplementary text provides overviews of major spheres in anthropology. In easy-to-read prose aimed at introductory-level students, this collection of essays offers accounts of the general frameworks that underlie anthropology.

Although this book is primarily aimed at students in basic, introductory, four-field anthropology classes—of any size—it can be used in any introductory level course in **cultural anthropology**, archaeology, biological anthropology, or a combination of archaeology (prehistory) and **bioanthropology**, the anthropology of our past. For the most part, the chapters affect any field: for example, ethics is important in cultural, archaeological, linguistic, or biological anthropology; there are patterns in all cultures, languages, tools, and fossils; theory is valuable to any subfield; and most anthropologists are scientists and construct their fieldwork to test hypotheses.

Although you can obviously assign chapters in consecutive order, each chapter stands alone, and you can mix them up or even ignore one or two. While we feel it is best to assign this book early in the term to get students thinking anthropologically from the beginning, say two chapters each session before launching into the "day's material," you can think of your own best use of the materials and modify your plan the next time if it seems warranted.

Chapter 2: **"What Anthropologists Look For: Patterns."** What are anthropologists looking for, and what counts as anthropological knowledge?

Chapter 3: **"Thinking Holistically."** What are the different subdivisions of anthropology, and how do their interrelationships contribute to anthropological knowledge and thinking?

Chapter 4: **"Thinking Theoretically."** What is theory, and what part does it play in anthropology?

Chapter 5: **"Using Science to Think Anthropologically."** What is science, and how can it be used in anthropology?

Chapter 6: **"Thinking About Change: Biological Evolution, Culture Change, and the Importance of Scale."** How can we think about and understand change?

Chapter 7: **"Why Do Anthropological Experts Disagree?"** Why do anthropologists disagree about evidence and interpretations?

Chapter 8: **"Thinking and Acting Ethically in Anthropology."** What does ethics have to do with anthropology, and why should we be concerned about ethics anyhow?

Chapter 9: **"Applying Anthropological Knowledge."** How is anthropological knowledge used in the real world?

Chapter 10: **"Making Ideas Researchable."** How do anthropologists define concepts and ideas in order to begin to think about researching them?

Chapter 11: **"Thinking Anthropologically About 'Race': Human Variation, Culture Construction, and Dispelling Myths."** How has the concept of "race" changed from basically biological to cultural in concept, and what are the implications of "cultural races"?

Chapter 12: **"Thinking with Gender."** What has feminist anthropology done to change anthropology and how we think anthropologically?

Chapter 13: **"Fieldwork: Collecting Information."** How do anthropologists in various subfields collect information about what it is to be human?

Chapter 14: **"How to Take Anthropology Tests."** How can students take anthropology tests and do well?

The discussions in *Thinking Anthropologically* provide an overview of anthropological thinking, helping students follow the material you are covering in your teaching and the substantive content in the main text or case studies that you use. *Thinking Anthropologically* relieves the introductory instructor of the need to cover these background frameworks while attempting to impart knowledge in the classroom. It gives students a ready reference in the areas that are likely to puzzle them.

Although instructors can assign individual chapters or the entire primer, as needed, we envision *Thinking Anthropologically* as a basic student aid in introductory courses. If your students learn to think anthropologically early on, they will better understand you and the major text you use, they will do better in the course, and they will appreciate anthropology more. We suggest assigning the book for the first week or two of class.

Finally, we ask you not only to assign this volume to your students but also to help us improve it. Which chapters were the most useful and which the least useful? Were there problems with individual chapters? Which other topics would you and your students like covered in a new edition? Please let us know. You can find both Philip Carl Salzman and Patricia Rice and our e-mail addresses in the American Anthropological Association Guide, available through www.aaanet.org. We would like to hear what you think.

STUDY QUESTIONS

1. You enrolled in this course before you read this book. Can you suggest one or two subjects you expected to learn about in this class? Write a paragraph about how you expect your thinking to change.
2. Like the co-editors of this book, Salzman with philosophy and Rice with economics, can you think of a college course you have taken where your interest and knowledge of that class would have increased if you had learned how to "think" the subject early on? In what ways would it have improved?

CHAPTER 2

What Anthropologists Look For: Patterns

Philip Carl Salzman

McGill University

When anthropologists study people, what are they looking for? What do they want to know, and how do they know when they know something? When you study people and peoples, and cultures and societies, what should you be looking for?

Archaeologists examine the remains of past cultures by sorting through pot shards, stone implements, and bones. They are looking for patterns of tool use, site occupation, and ritual activity. Physical and biological anthropologists study the human body, its variations, and commonalities within and between populations. They are looking for patterns of interaction between environments and genetic populations and between populations. Linguists focus on language as a coherent system and as an integral part of culture and society. They are looking for patterns of language commonality or variation in relation to social life and cultural orientations. **Sociocultural** anthropologists talk to people about their ideas and values, observe people as they go about their lives, and monitor their activities. They are looking for patterns in belief and value, in the conjunction of ideas and actions, and in the relationship between different practices and institutions.

What would you be looking for if you were faced with an opportunity like the one I had doing my first ethnographic field research? I remember driving slowly across the desert in Baluchistan, in southeastern Iran, dodging the small sand dunes as our Land Rover approached a line of black goat hair tents, the home of a herding group of Baluchi tribal nomads. We were approached by a dignified, bearded man of middle age wearing a turban, baggy trousers, and a long shirt hanging to his knees. My wife and I waited while our companion, the charming brother of the tribal chief, got out to explain to this amazed camp headman that we wanted to live with him and his community. Soon thereafter, we were setting up our baby blue canvas exoskeleton tent (totally unsuitable for local conditions, as it turned out) near the tent of the headman, Jafar. Once our household was set up and we had begun to figure out how to live in a tent in the desert, I turned my attention to research.

One main thing I wanted to know was how these Baluchi nomads made a living amid the sand dunes. Of course, I was not starting from zero, from complete ignorance, because I had read about Middle Eastern and Iranian nomads and had some idea what I was likely to find in Baluchistan. So I was not alone in my research; I relied on anthropological ideas and ethnographic information provided by anthropologists (and historians and travelers) who had thought about these problems and done research before me. (Anthropology is a collective project in other, parallel ways: educational institutions train new anthropologists and provide jobs; public and private funding agencies provide the money needed for research.)

PATTERNS IN MAKING A LIVING

Middle Eastern nomads, as we know them from previous studies done in the twentieth century, made a living (at least partly) by raising livestock: sheep, goats, and camels. Some, such as the Rwala Bedouin (Lancaster 1997) of northern Arabia, raised mainly camels; some, such as the Basseri of southwestern Iran (Barth 1961), raised mainly sheep; the Baluchi nomads (Salzman 2000), as I discovered in the course of my research, raised mainly goats but sheep also (two goats for each sheep) and had a small number of camels.

This is our first example of what anthropologists look for: *patterns in the life of a human population or group.* **Pattern** in anthropology and social science more generally means a repetition of a social or cultural phenomenon—a belief, a practice, a custom, or an institution—over space or time. For example, that Middle Eastern nomads raised livestock (as distinct from some nomads elsewhere, who hunt for a living) on natural pasture (**pastoralism**) is a pattern; that different groups of nomads raised different animal species (or in markedly different ratios) is another pattern.

What about **nomadism**? Why did these nomads move their households and community groups regularly? Mainly they moved to accommodate their livestock; they moved to find the best pasture and water for their animals and to avoid disease, predators, and enemies. But not all nomads followed the same *pattern of migration.* The Basseri (Barth 1961) migrated in a fairly regular way between mountain summer pastures and lowland winter pastures. In contrast, the Baluch (Salzman 2000) moved first one way and then another, in an irregular fashion, the pattern changing each year. What was predictable about the Baluchi migration pattern was that it was unpredictable. Different nomadic groups had different migration patterns.

The patterns we have discussed so far are *descriptive* in that they report a characteristic of a particular population or group. When I say "they mostly had camels," that is a descriptive pattern of *central tendency*, a kind of average. It tells you the main thing but not everything. When I say, "they had a 2:1 ratio of goats to sheep and some camels as well," the descriptive pattern is one of *distribution*, indicating not only the main thing but the more minor things as well.

Descriptive patterns are answers to the question "What is present here?" But anthropologists also ask "Why is this pattern present here?" Another kind of pattern, *associational patterns*, which show how some characteristics are associated with other characteristics, are (at least partial) answers to the "Why?" question.

For example, if we investigate why some Middle Eastern nomads herded sheep, some herded goats, and others herded camels, we will discover that there is an association between the kind of livestock herded and the environment, particularly the climate. The nomads who herded mainly sheep lived in more humid environments (10 or more inches of rainfall), whereas those who herded mainly goats lived in arid environments (5 inches of rainfall a year), and those who herded mainly camels lived in very arid environments (less than 3 inches of rainfall a year).

Similarly, migration patterns are also associated with aridity. Nomads such as the Basseri, who migrated regularly and predictably between summer and winter pastures seasonally, lived in more humid environments, whereas nomads such as the Rwala Bedouin and the Baluch, who lived in more arid environments, followed erratic and irregular migration patterns to find pasture and water wherever it was available. This relationship between migration and climate, like the relationship between livestock species and climate, is an associational pattern, which shows that certain characteristics go together or are correlated.

Another aspect of the Baluchi nomadic economy quickly caught my attention. I went to Baluchistan hoping to study nomads who did nothing but raise livestock, who were called "pure" nomads by some anthropologists. When I confided this to the tribal chief, he appeared to have no idea what I was talking about. The reason was that all Baluchi nomads were involved in several different sectors of production. Yes, Baluchi men raised livestock, but they also cultivated date palms, engaged in small-scale grain cultivation, occasionally hunted and gathered, and, in the past, engaged in predatory raiding of peasants and caravans, but more recently many left the tribal territory to work for money or engage in trade. We can sum up this descriptive pattern by saying that the Baluchi economy was not specialized, focused on one product, but was rather mixed or multiresource, distributed among several spheres of production.

Why did some nomads, such as the Rwala Bedouin and the Basseri, specialize in economic production, putting most of their efforts into their livestock, whereas other nomads, such as the Baluch and the Nuer (Evans-Pritchard 1940) of the southern Sudan, were committed to cultivating, raiding, trading, or, in the case of the Nuer, who raised cattle in a very humid environment, fishing. Are specialized livestock breeding and mixed or multiresource production associated with different circumstances?

In general, nomads who had multiresource economies had them because of their consumption practices: they were subsistence oriented, producing goods for their own consumption. For this reason, they had to produce a range of products—milk, meat, wool, hair, leather, and also grain, dates, green vegetables, and, where applicable, fish—to provide a full diet and raw materials for what they need to make, such as goat hair for tents and wool for clothes and luggage bags. The Baluch and Nuer lived on what they produced, so they had to produce everything they needed.

In contrast, nomadic peoples who had specialized economies had them because they were market oriented, planned to sell their livestock in the market and to purchase whatever consumption goods they needed in the market. While the Rwala were herding their camels deep in the empty deserts of northern Arabia they were thinking about the urban markets that would buy their camels to supply the caravan trade. Similarly, the Basseri trekking with their sheep through the high Zagros Mountains of Iran were planning to sell them in the bazaar of the garden city of Shiraz and buy clothes, grain, dried vegetables, tea, and sugar there.

The associational pattern we have identified here is that nomads specialized in pastoral production of livestock when they could sell animals in the marketplace and could buy their consumption goods with the money they received, whereas nomads who relied on what they produced for consumption had multiresource economies to provide them with the necessary range of products.

The nomadic, pastoral, multiresource *pattern of land use* that I saw when I was doing research in Baluchistan had been present for at least 100 years. But was it always the pattern of land use in that part of Baluchistan? This question can be answered only through evidence about what happened in the past and through time. In the absence of accessible historical records, we turn to anthropological archaeologists to answer this question. Archaeologists examine the physical remains of the past to discover patterns existing in different periods. An archaeological survey of the area of Baluchistan I studied shows impressive remains from the past, remains that demonstrate definitively that in the past a totally different pattern of land use was dominant.

Across today's desert landscape are seen what might look like rows of bomb craters: a line of holes each surrounded by a rim of soil. But these are the surface manifestations of *qanat*, underground water tunnels for irrigation. Each hole and rim mark the place where soil was removed to make the tunnel and where workers entered the tunnel to maintain it. *Qanat*, sometimes 10 or more kilometers long, begin at a point where the mother well taps the water table at an altitude higher than the place to be irrigated, and gravity brings the water downhill until it comes to the surface at the irrigation site.

The archaeological survey mentioned earlier, finding 73 *qanat* remains, shows that prior to the last century of nomadic land use, irrigation **agriculture** was dominant in this region. Irrigation agriculture requires the ongoing presence of cultivators to distribute the water to the crops in a precise and systematic fashion. To do this, and to protect the crops, the cultivators would have had to be mainly sedentary. Thus, thanks to archaeological analysis, we now know that the pattern of land use in this area of Baluchistan has changed markedly over time. The shift from irrigation agriculture to nomadic pastoralism and multiresource exploitation identifies an important *historical pattern* for this region.

PATTERNS IN MARRIAGE, FAMILY, AND COMMUNITY

Among the Baluchi nomads, the family was more important than in industrial America and Europe. The reason for this is clear: families and their associated households not only provided a residence, a place for the consumption of food, biological reproduction, and the socialization and enculturation of children, but also were the unit of economic production, in which all the things people needed were produced.

A new family and a new household were formed by marriage, and the position of that family among others was determined by the kinship ties of each partner to his or her parents, siblings, and other relatives. Marriages, especially first marriages, usually were arranged by parents, with the consent of the engaged couple. Whom did the Baluchi nomads marry?

As in much of the Middle East, Baluchi nomads preferred to marry close relatives. "Marry a cousin and you know what you are getting," they told me. And when they say "what you are getting," they were considering not only the spouse, whose character and abilities were well understood, but also parents-in-law, brothers-in-law, and all relatives by marriage, with whom one would be closely involved. The Baluch preferred patrilateral, parallel cousin marriage, that is, marriage to one's father's brother's children. Why did the Baluch and other Middle Eastern nomads favor the father's brother's children over the mother's brother's or father's sister's children? The reason for this is clear: Baluchi nomads, like all other Middle Eastern nomads, reckoned descent through the male line and organized important defense and cooperation groups in terms of descent through a common male ancestor. By marrying your father's brother's child, you would be certain of marrying a member of your own defense group within which solidarity and support were expected. Your in-laws would be members of your defense group. Such marriages thus led to maximum solidarity in both the family and the defense group.

The preference that one marry close, and marry close patrilineal kin if possible, is a descriptive pattern, like specializing in goats. But whereas the animals one specializes in are described by a *statistical pattern*, the injunction to marry close is a **normative pattern** because it is felt to be the right thing to do and forms a rule of behavior. Baluch would not say you are wrong to specialize in sheep (although they might say you were unwise), but they would say you are wrong for disdaining close marriages and seeking distant ones. But even the normative pattern of marriage alliance is a **preferential** normative pattern, in that it is not obligatory. What if one looked to marry close, but there were no potential partners because everyone close and unmarried was too young or too old? Or maybe one's father did not have a brother, or his brother did not have a child of the appropriate gender or age. In such a case, marrying a more distant person would not be condemned. (The distance can be smoothed over semantically by referring to a second, third, or fourth cousin in a "classificatory" fashion as "my cousin" or "my father's brother's child" even though he or she is really one's father's father's brother's son's child.)

Such preferential normative patterns can be distinguished from *mandatory* or obligatory normative patterns, such as taking care of your children and not abusing your spouse. These are strict rules, and breaking them could not be justified; condemnation by public opinion would have been swift and sure. Another mandatory rule was that if a member of your lineage defense group was being attacked, you must go and defend that person as if you yourself were being attacked. Anthropologists call this rule collective responsibility, in which each member is obliged to act with total solidarity with all of the others, in the spirit of "all for one and one for all." (The North Atlantic Treaty Organization, NATO, has a similar rule, in which an attack on one member country is to be regarded as an attack on all.)

But normative rules are one thing, and humans' actions often are another thing. American parents commonly impose rules on their children against smoking, drinking, driving fast, and premarital intimacies. Notwithstanding the mandatory nature of these norms, young people often conduct their lives beyond the sight of their parents with disregard for such rules. Therefore, in addition to knowing the normative pattern, we need to look at the statistical or behavioral pattern as well, so that we can see how many people follow the rule and how many do not follow it. In Middle Eastern societies, although most people married not-too-distant relatives, only about 10 percent of marriages were between real patrilateral, parallel cousins; in communities with the best record, no more than half achieved this ideal (Barth 1954).

Similarly with mandatory normative patterns, the statistical pattern of actual behavior commonly shows a few people who violate the norm, who do not turn up to help their lineage mates, who do beat their wives, and who do not take care of their children. In response to these violations, the community generally takes some punitive measures, from verbal condemnation, through withdrawal of support, to expulsion. Anthropologists view these punitive measures as part of the *pattern of social control* through which a population maintains a set of rules and standards and thus a particular, cultural way of doing things.

When I describe the Middle Eastern marriage pattern, students often say, "Yikes! Marry my cousin? No way!" And then they ask whether Middle Easterners have deformities from marrying their cousins. This question takes us into the realm of biological anthropology. Framed more generally, the question is about an associational pattern: are marriages between close relatives associated with biological deformities or other negative consequences? In general, we can say that marriage between relatives is associated with deleterious effects only when a particular *genetic pattern* is present: a deleterious, recessive gene. In this case, the negative characteristic appears only at the phenotype (or external, bodily) level when two individuals, both with the recessive gene, contribute that gene to offspring. When such a deleterious recessive gene is present in a family line, the chances of two recessive genes coming together is greater if people are marrying close relatives. If both partners carry the recessive gene, 25 percent of their offspring will show the deleterious effect. Whether a given population increases the risk of negative consequences from marriage with relatives depends on their genetic pattern. (Of course, there may be social benefits from marriage with relatives that might outweigh such biological risks, should they exist.)

PATTERNS IN SOCIAL CONTROL AND POLITICS

Among the nomadic tribes of Baluchistan, security and defense were the responsibility of corporate lineage groups, groups defined by common descent through the male line. These lineage groups did not exist all of the time, for two reasons.

First, each tribesman and tribeswoman belonged to lineages of different sizes, depending on which ancestor one was counting from. A grandfather was the founder of a small microlineage, a great-grandfather was the founder of a larger minor lineage, and a great-great-grandfather was the founder of a fairly large medium lineage, and so on up to tribal sections, whole tribes, and sometimes tribal confederacies. However, whether the members of a lineage were called together to form an action group for defense depended on circumstances, particularly a threat to life or property. Which lineage became relevant at a particular moment and became activated, which lineage a tribesman thought about and counted himself a member of, depended on the opposing group threatening one's security. If a conflict broke out between close relatives, then each would gather the members of his microlineage to help him. If those in conflict were distant genealogically, then they would call on their medium or macrolineages to support them. So whether a given Baluch thought of himself as a member of the Shadi Hanzai microlineage or a member of the Soherabzai macrolineage depended on the circumstances, specifically who his opponent was. Anthropologists call such groups **contingent groups** in that they are called into existence and action only in response to certain circumstances, or contingencies.

The second reason that these defense groups did not exist all of the time was that people did not engage in security and defensive activities all of the time. Unlike our police officers, soldiers, and firefighters, who put on their uniforms and go to work each day, all men in a Baluchi tribe are members of lineage defense groups at the same time as they are herders, cultivators, traders, and nomads. Members of a lineage defense group live in different residential communities. So when defense matters arise, lineage members must be activated; the Baluch must drop whatever they are doing and come together to decide what actions to take.

The pattern of contingency (or its opposite, permanence) in action groups can be called a *meta-pattern* in that it applies to many specific descriptive patterns. Meta-patterns can also be found in historical and prehistorical patterns, that is, over time, as the following examples indicate.

Among the Baluchi tribes and elsewhere, existing social and cultural patterns are not all of equal strength: some are strongly manifest whereas others are weaker, or latent. On a day-to-day basis in Baluchistan, people may be focusing on raising their livestock and growing their crops, not thinking about security and defense. At this moment, defense groups are latent. When a serious conflict arises, people organize into defense groups, which then become manifest. This is what is meant by contingent pattern.

We see a similar latent/manifest alternation in the two main Baluchi political institutions, the lineages and the tribal chiefship. Lineages come to the fore as opponents during conflict; the tribal chief comes to the fore as a mediator stressing peace and trying to reestablish unity.

This contingency can also exist over long historical periods. During periods of strife, lineage affiliation and defense groups are manifest and central. During such times, other foci, such as religion, tend to recede and weaken. But during periods of peace, religion, in the Baluchi case Sunni Islam, can be activated as a major concern and focus of activity. In this way, there can be an alternation over time, with religion strongly manifest and lineage defense groups latent for a period, whereas in another period lineage defense groups are strongly manifest and religion weak and latent.

To take another example, during periods of political independence, Baluchi tribesmen were active and enthusiastic predatory raiders, robbing caravans and distant villages. Once conquered and encapsulated by the Iranian state in 1935, the tribesmen turned their energies and creativity to (among other things) expanding their limited agricultural cultivation. Even irrigation technology, long out of use in the region, was reactivated. This meta-pattern of alternation through prehistoric and historical time is widespread and can be seen in many specific patterns.

CONCLUSION

What anthropologists look for in studying culture and society is *patterns in the life of a human population or group*. This includes, among many others, patterns of land use, patterns of movement, production patterns, marriage patterns, and defense cooperation patterns.

One main kind of pattern that anthropologists seek, especially in ethnographic field research, is *descriptive patterns* that convey many important characteristics of the particular society and culture being studied. Descriptive patterns can report a *central tendency*, one or another form of average (for example, Baluchi nomadic households contain on average 6.3 individuals); alternatively, a *distributional pattern* reports the range of cases (for example, Baluchi nomadic households range from 2 to 13 individuals, with the second and third quartiles ranging from 4.6 to 7.2 individuals).

One kind of descriptive pattern is a *historical pattern* that reports changes in human activity, such as in land use pattern, over time. One *meta-pattern* that we have seen is the alternation of specific cultural patterns through time (such as lineage and chiefly dominance, or conflict and religion in Baluchistan) in both short-term and long, historical cycles.

The number of individuals in a household is a *statistical pattern* or *behavioral pattern*, as is the percentage of people praying every day or the number of people who prefer to herd sheep rather than goats. Another kind of pattern is the *normative pattern*, a rule or moral obligation, such as helping lineage mates among the Baluch or abstaining from sexual relations outside of marriage. Normative patterns can be *preferential* in that the rule is regarded as a good thing to follow (such as marrying a close relative) or *mandatory* (such as joining with lineage mates to take vengeance on attackers from another lineage).

When we are examining the relationship between two descriptive patterns, we might discover an *associational pattern* that illustrates that two descriptive patterns are co-related or correlated with one another and tend to appear together. Examples include the association between regular migration patterns and regular, predictable climates, and between irregular migration patterns and irregular, unpredictable climates, and the association between subsistence-oriented production and multiresource economies, and between market-oriented production and specialized economies.

REFERENCES

BARTH, FREDRIK
    1954. "Father's Brother's Daughter Marriage in Kurdistan." *Southwestern Journal of Anthropology* 10: 164–171.
    1961. *Nomads of South Persia.* Oslo: Oslo University Press.
EVANS-PRITCHARD E. E.
    1940. *The Nuer.* Oxford: The Clarendon Press.
LANCASTER, WILLIAM
    1997. *The Rwala Bedouin Today* (2nd edition). Prospect Heights, IL: Waveland.
SALZMAN, PHILIP CARL
    2000. *Black Tents of Baluchistan.* Washington, DC: Smithsonian Institution Press.

STUDY QUESTIONS

1. In what ways is American culture like that of the Baluch in economics and getting a living?
2. In what ways is American culture different from the Baluch in social organization?
3. Make a list of at least three patterns of culture in American culture having to do with social control.

3

Thinking Holistically

Holly Peters-Golden
University of Michigan

Whether the course you are taking is an introductory anthropology class addressing all of the subdisciplines (biological anthropology, cultural anthropology, archaeology, and linguistic anthropology) or one that focuses on one of these fields, chances are you will begin with a discussion of **holism**. Holism is a central defining concept in anthropology, one that sets it apart from other disciplines that study humanity. What is holism? Why is it such a critical feature of anthropology? Finally, why do anthropologists think holistically?

When used in a general sense, holism might be most familiarly represented by the expression "the whole is greater than the sum of its parts." In adding up all the particulars, the end result is something more than—and different from—those constituent elements. This is true for an individual human being, who is certainly more than the sum of biological traits and cultural knowledge; it is also true for an entire society, which is not merely a collection of individual members (Schultz and Lavenda 2008).

The *holistic perspective in anthropology* tries to take into consideration all aspects of human life, as found throughout time and across space. Holism is the "study of the whole of the human condition: past, present, and future; biology, science, language, and culture" (Kottak 2009). Through cross-cultural comparative studies, we can recognize both the great diversity among peoples as well as the human characteristics that unite us all. Anthropologists don't generalize about "human nature" or "the way people are" without taking into consideration a wide range of different societies. However, it is not sufficient merely to cast a wide enough net to capture all the varied features of human life. We cannot accurately represent anthropology by defining it as being made up of biological, cultural, linguistic, and archaeological aspects, lined up side by side. It is the ways in which all these aspects are integrated, the elegant ways in which they influence one another, which exemplify anthropology's holistic perspective.

Speaking literally, holism is something of an ideal. Whatever anthropology's best intentions, it is impossible to know everything about all of humanity. The depth and breadth of human existence are vast. Human beings and their cultures are complex and changing; we are continually learning new facts and revising old assumptions. Yet anthropology strives to maintain the holistic perspective on several levels, recognizing that each part of culture is connected to and influenced by the other parts and by the whole, that the past is connected to the present (and the future), and that each of the four subdisciplines is inextricably bound to the others.

The essence of thinking anthropologically is "thinking holistically." What follow in this chapter are examples of holism, both between the subdisciplines and within each subdiscipline, designed to help you begin to recognize the process of asking questions, making comparisons, weighing alternatives, and looking at the study of humankind the way anthropologists do: holistically.

HOLISM: CONNECTIONS WITHIN CULTURES

The concept of culture is central to anthropology and central to the holistic perspective. Culture, the learned beliefs and behaviors characteristic of a particular group, can provide the organizing framework for demonstrating the ways in which the varied aspects of human life—art, politics, religion, marriage, family, economics, and medicine, to name a few—are *interdependent*. The economic system of a society influences the meaning of a marriage alliance; food production is tied to political systems. Gender roles can vary in relation to economic systems; religious rituals may serve environmental ends. Art can reflect social oppression; illness beliefs can grow out of gender stereotypes. The holistic perspective begins with the assumption that cultures are *integrated systems* that contain recognizable patterns of belief and behavior, threads woven into a larger fabric of meaning and practice. However, culture is not a restrictive mandate to be followed blindly, nor is it one rigid set of rules without alternatives. People often challenge cultural rules and negotiate change in an active, creative way.

On a more complex level, the imbalance of birth rates between boys and girls in parts of rural China provides a powerful example of the *interrelationship* of politics, economics, kinship, law, family structure, and medical technology. Decades ago, in an attempt to stem overpopulation, the Chinese government instituted a policy that mandated no more than one child per couple. Those who violate this rule are subject to fines. Some wealthy people are able to shoulder the economic burden of stiff fines, but most rural villagers cannot. In much of rural China, daughters move at marriage to live with their husband's family, and it is sons on whom the financial security of the family rests. Moreover, in the absence of government health care, elderly parents depend on sons to care for them in their old age. Recently, inexpensive prenatal scans have become available to pregnant villagers, and despite laws against such screening, they are used to determine the sex of a fetus, with the result that females are sometimes aborted. Recent census data show that the worldwide average birth ratio is 106 boys to 100 girls, whereas in 2005, China's national average was 119 boys to 100 girls; in some parts of the countryside, the ratio was 144:100. The marital consequences of China's "missing girls" are already in evidence, with reports of women being abducted and sold to men who cannot find wives, seen by the villagers as a disastrous economic and cultural situation (Eckholm 2002). Alarmed by the selective abortion of females, Chinese officials and scholars have recognized the ways many aspects of rural village life—government mandates, poverty, gaps in health care, gender bias, and many others—act together, and the government has begun to mount programs to address the problem holistically, knowing that one cultural phenomenon will affect the others.

HOLISM: CONNECTIONS ACROSS THE FOUR FIELDS

Despite the widely shared holistic perspective that guides anthropologists to examine the whole range of human life, the discipline of anthropology is generally divided into four areas of study: cultural anthropology, biological anthropology, archaeology, and linguistic anthropology. However, each subfield illuminates related issues in the others.

The beginnings of American anthropology, roughly 100 years ago, grew out of an interest in the history and culture of the peoples native to North America. The questions early anthropologists asked about the diverse indigenous peoples of North America spanned what we now identify as the four fields or subdisciplines. **Native Americans** spoke different languages, had different social structures and different customs in general, differed in physical appearance, and perhaps had different origins. Once the reservation system was in place, it was generally feared that these cultures would disappear, spurring American anthropologists to do all they could to preserve at least a record of as much as possible. Anthropologists attempted to study every aspect of native language, culture, artifacts, and physical features (Bourguignon 1996). Thus, the holistic perspective in America is rooted in the very inception of the discipline of anthropology.

Perhaps the best way to demonstrate the principle of holism across the discipline of anthropology is to examine the ways in which the four areas of inquiry are interconnected.

Archaeology Connects

When students think of **archaeology**, what often comes to mind are things rather than people: shards of pottery, bits of animal bones, and stones shaped into weapons and tools. A cultural anthropologist can ask questions of a group of people to learn about their culture, but how can an archaeologist get answers to questions about the past? Rather than *observe* behavior the way cultural anthropologists do, archaeologists *reconstruct* behavior through their study of material remains. The grandest pyramid and the smallest grain of fossilized pollen can "speak" to an archaeologist. Cultural anthropologists provide a wealth of information about people all over the world, but their study of society and culture generally cannot reach back beyond several hundred years. Archaeology can reveal ways of life that are no longer observable and provide an understanding of long-term cultural change (Jolly and White 1995). Here, the link is between the past and the present as well as between two anthropological subfields.

The material remains that have been left behind can illuminate cultural patterns in the past, but are they holistic patterns? Archaeologists can determine whether groups of people were food gatherers or food cultivators and whether the animals they consumed were wild or domesticated, thereby providing insights into ancient economies. By examining artifacts—materials that people have made or modified in some way—we may learn about many aspects of prehistoric life. Discerning what prehistoric peoples ate may seem unimportant, but as archaeologist Robert Ehrenreich (1996) points out, myriad other questions and issues arise out of inquiry into diet. For example, how did diet change over time, and why? What role did food play in population size? How was food secured and prepared, and by whom? What sort of rituals or aesthetics surrounded food? How might diet provide information about social organization, beliefs about health, prestige, celebration, or division of labor? These suggest that archaeologists do seek holistic patterns because diet appears to have been closely related to social organization, social roles, art, ritual, and economics in the past just as it is in the present.

Consider the cultural information archaeologists can provide through just one kind of artifact: potsherds, or fragments of pottery. The quantity of pottery bits found at a site might indicate the population size. Materials used in making pottery but not found locally point toward trading activities. At different sites, the discovery of pots that are similar in various features may be a result of cultural connections (Kottak 2009). Archaeologists contribute to our understanding of ecology, the ways states and cities arise, economic and social organization, and even gender roles. In addition to contributions to our understanding of prehistory, archaeologists also provide insights into recent history and modern peoples. For example, archaeologists excavating sites in the American South are reconstructing the lifeways of eighteenth-century slaves transported from Africa to work on plantations. Previously, information about the diet, clothing, and possessions of slave families was gathered through the manifests of their owners. Written records kept by plantation owners detailed meals and material goods furnished to slaves; the "ethnographic record" was akin to the inventory in a store. The list of foods provided for slaves was assumed to be an accurate representation of foods the slaves ate; clothing and household items given to them were recorded as their possessions. However, archaeological excavation of the slave quarters shows an entirely different, very rich culture. Bones of small game that were hunted on a regular basis are evidence of a supplemented diet; pottery and baskets were fashioned for decoration and utility. Also unearthed were game pieces such as homemade dominoes and a variety of musical instruments. The material remains archaeologists find can rewrite **ethnography**.

In its discovery and interpretation of past environments and inhabitants, archaeology is also connected to biological anthropology. Archaeologists and biological anthropologists share many of the same concepts and techniques in their mutual study of humanity's past (Schultz and Lavenda 2008). Biological anthropologists who study the fossil record of human evolution work closely with archaeologists to reveal a picture of the human past that is both biological and cultural. For example, the position of **Neandertal** in our human ancestry is contentious at best and probably will continue to be so in the future. Biological anthropologists compare populations in existence before and particularly after Neandertals existed in Europe and the Near East to assess the possibility of evolutionary connections; archaeologists compare artifacts before and after Neandertal in the same areas to assess the possibility of cultural connections between populations that would show up in artifact similarities. We will never be able to conclude whether Neandertal had anything to do with our ancestry unless we look at both the biology and culture of that population and the modern one that succeeded it. Significant differences in **DNA** and artifacts may lead us to discount Neandertal's place in our ancestry; similarities in biological traits and culture traditions may instead point toward a connection.

Although language doesn't fossilize, archaeological evidence can still shed some light on this topic. Increasing complexity in tools and other artifacts corresponds with increasing brain complexity, one part of which is the development of language and speech. In the argument about when complex language originated, some say it was a result of a great increase in cultural abilities. Other researchers look at cultural accomplishments documented in the archaeological record, including bone tools, complex stone-tool traditions, cave art, and burials, and ask whether they would all be possible without language already being in place. One interesting experiment attempted to show when speech might have been necessary in tool manufacturing. An expert in flint toolmaking taught a group of students how to make **handaxes** by imitation; they did exactly what the expert did, and each successfully made a simple handaxe, a tool commonly manufactured between 2.6 million and 40 thousand years ago. They could also make flake tools by watching the instructor hit the edge of the flake with a hammerstone. However, the students were totally unsuccessful at making blade tools using only imitation. Blade tool manufacture, which became the norm starting about 40 thousand years ago, apparently demands oral instruction for success (Bernard 1980).

Linguistic Anthropology Connects

Despite the fact that we do not know when our human ancestors began to *speak*, we do know that language (whether spoken or signed) is central to being human. The reach of linguistic anthropology, the study of language in its cultural context, extends across time and place and also extends to the other fields of anthropology.

A central theme in holistic anthropology is the recognition of both the diversity of humanity and the commonalities that underpin it. Language is a vehicle for demonstrating at the same time the universal and the particular in human life: all humans share the capacity for language, but there is a rich diversity in the several thousand languages about which we have data. This linguistic diversity correlates with cultural diversity (Hickerson 1997).

Language is at the heart of the way we engage with each other and with the world around us. Through language, children learn the intricacies of their culture to become members of their society. In learning a group's language, we learn more than words, grammar, and pronunciation; we learn about the culture in which that language is used. The centrality of this tenet is reflected in the fact that cultural anthropologists conduct their fieldwork in the language of the people among whom they are working. Early linguistic anthropologist Edward Sapir wrote in 1912, "The worlds in which different societies live are distinct worlds, not merely the same world with different labels attached" (as quoted by Bonvillain 1997:49).

As the vehicle through which we think, communicate, and organize our beliefs about the way the world works, language can provide insights into culture. Linguistic anthropologists study a variety of features of language, such as structure, history, sound, change, meaning, acquisition, and use. Each of these can illuminate assumptions, values, and interests of the wider culture in which the language is found. For example, language can reveal social inequality through hierarchical differences in terms of address, greetings, pronouns, and kinship terms. Speakers of a language can convey distance, solidarity, respect, collegiality, superiority, class, and power by choosing from among various titles, names, and expressions. Japanese society is stratified in terms of class, gender, and age, with deference shown to wealthy people and those in high-status jobs, to men, and to the elderly. Many features of the Japanese language reflect these differences in status, with choice of words, titles, grammatical constructions, and tone directed by the relative rank of those conversing (Bonvillain 1997).

By comparing the speech of men and women in a variety of social settings, linguistic anthropologists have demonstrated numerous differences in language use. Men and women have been shown to use different vocabularies, styles of speech, grammar, and tone. Gendered patterns of speech reflect social roles of women and men, exemplifying "proper" behavior as well as defining the realms in which they are expected to have knowledge.

The lexicon of a language—its inventory of words—is another connection between language and culture. The stock of words exemplifies what is important to a group. Think of the explosion of terms and expressions linked to computers and cyberspace that has occurred in recent years. Foragers and horticulturalists can name far more plants than people in industrial societies; residents of the Arctic have words to describe variations in ice and snow that people in temperate climates could never distinguish (Kottak 2009). Similar examples can be found in sports terms, colors, foods, types of animals, and more: Serena Nanda and Rich Warms (2007) report that residents of Munich, Germany, have more than seventy words to describe the color, strength, carbonation, and other qualities of beer.

Language can be a powerful tool for both domination and resistance. Throughout history, people have felt and expressed their identity through language. Its importance is demonstrated by the fact that political and social oppression often includes the mandate that a group give up its own language. Resistance to such an edict is a vehicle for rebellion and sometimes takes very clever form: when Chinese authorities attempted to prevent the Hmong ethnic minority from speaking their own language, Hmong women, who are renowned textile artists, devised a pictorial code that they appliquéd to their skirts, sending messages to one another and making fun of their oppressors (Willcox 1986).

The link between language and culture may be obvious, but the study of language is relevant to archaeology and biological anthropology as well. Historical linguistics studies the development and change of language over time. Changes, differences, and similarities across languages can indicate common origins as well as contact through marriage, trade relations, and even war. Historical linguists have worked with archaeologists to trace the spread of particular technologies and material culture by linking them to the spread of language (Scupin and DeCorse 2008).

Language and human origins have a connection that is basic to anthropology: our elaboration of and dependence on language often is cited as one of the defining features that makes us human. Biological anthropologists are interested in the development and evolution of the capacities for human language in the brain and speech via the vocal anatomy. Language is a bridge between the biological and cultural aspects of humanity, demonstrating their interconnectedness.

In addition to investigating the beginnings of language in humans, biological anthropologists compare communication systems among humans and nonhuman primates. There is much controversy over the interpretation of results of studies teaching apes to use sign language and other forms of symbolic communication. However, it seems clear that in many aspects the differences between humans and apes are not as great as was previously believed. Given that humans and apes share common ancestry, when did our communicative abilities begin to differ (Relethford 2007)? When did we begin to speak?

Biological Anthropology Connects

Whereas some anthropologists are concerned primarily with cultural beliefs and practices and others focus on *biological evolution* and *modern human variation,* all anthropologists would agree that the essence of being human is grounded in the interconnection of biology and culture. We are biological organisms, with both needs and limitations dictated by that nature. But we are cultural beings as well, and it is our ability to learn and our capacity for culture that set us apart from other animals. Human biology and human culture are engaged in an elegant dance that has spanned all the times and places of human existence. The transformative interaction of biology and culture is demonstrated by referring to humankind as biocultural.

As we examine the evolution of humanity, we see biological and cultural changes often working together. It was the combination of advances in both biology and culture that allowed us to continue to evolve and thrive. Anatomical changes in locomotion allowed early humans to travel greater distances to gather and hunt more efficiently. More sophisticated tool kits resulted in further successful exploitation of the environment. Changes in technology—culture—often resulted in anatomical changes. Tools that could cut, grind, and mash food took much of the burden off jaws and chewing muscles. With less work to do, jaws reduced in size. Because large teeth cannot fit in smaller jaws, **natural selection** favored smaller teeth as well.

Anatomical demands also had cultural consequences. Walking upright requires a compact pelvis to provide sufficient support. However, larger skull size (for larger brains) necessitates a wider birth canal. The balance struck by natural selection is the birth of children at a time when they can fit through the pelvic canal, but a time when they are immature and greatly dependent on their parents and community for their care. Thus, biological and anatomical aspects of evolution directly influence social life, with immature offspring needing years of nurturance, protection, and teaching.

Human health and illness provide another example of the interrelationship of biology and culture, both in modern times and in the past. Different methods of securing food and different types of social organization leave populations vulnerable to different sorts of illnesses. Small, mobile groups of foragers rarely experience epidemics of infectious disease. Limited population size curbs high rates of infection, and moving from site to site limits problems caused by poor sanitation and contaminated water supplies. In agricultural societies, however, populations are larger and sedentary, allowing infectious diseases to take hold. Cultural practices such as the use of domesticated animals to help in the fields increase exposure to potentially contaminated waste products. Industrialization brings its own health risks and benefits.

In modern times, we see powerful ways in which cultural and social factors are brought to bear on biological well-being. Improved sanitation, immunization, insect control, and antibiotics are all cultural innovations that have had positive effects. However, poverty, pollution, discrimination, war, environmental change, and lack of access to health care have dire physiological consequences. Both biology and culture are factors in disease; likewise, disease has effects that are both biological and social. The current AIDS epidemic not only has sickened and killed millions but also has profoundly changed the fabric of society in a variety of ways. AIDS has engendered fear and discrimination, inspired scientific research and humanitarianism, restructured households and communities, and rewritten laws and literature.

Cultural Anthropology Connects

Culture is a central concept of anthropology, and *cultural anthropologists* investigate the diversity of belief and behavior across societies. However, as we have seen, this subdiscipline is connected to and dependent on the other three.

Cultural rules differ from biological laws, but culture has the power to shape human biology. Conrad Kottak (2009) describes the ways in which culture acts as an environmental force to sculpt the human form. Culture differentially encourages some activities and abilities and discourages others. For example, particular sports result in very distinctive physical development. Cultural standards of beauty often mitigate against participation. Kottak suggests that Brazilian women avoid competitive swimming largely because it produces a bulky, muscular body type that runs counter to the ideal of Brazilian female beauty, which is softer and more curvaceous.

The choice of mates is another way in which culture influences biology. Learned preferences and cultural rules influence gene frequencies when individuals select or avoid particular partners, mating with individuals of the same height or with different hair color.

A classic example of the interaction between culture and biology is that of the sickle cell gene. **Sickle cell anemia**, a condition in which the red blood cells are misshapen and unable to deliver oxygen efficiently, is a potentially fatal disease. Healthy individuals possess two alleles for normal hemoglobin, the oxygen transport protein in red blood cells. Those with sickle cell anemia have two alleles for the abnormal hemoglobin. Scientists were surprised to find populations in Africa, India, and the Mediterranean with high frequencies of one abnormal hemoglobin allele until it was determined that although having two alleles for sickle cells was disastrous, having only one acted as protection against malaria. The geographic distribution of the sickle cell trait is very close to that of malaria. In malarial environments, it is advantageous to have one abnormal allele rather than two normal ones. In the early 1970s, biological anthropologist Frank Livingstone, seeking to explain the distribution of the sickle cell trait, demonstrated the ways in which culture played a role in shaping this genetic picture. Thousands of years ago, the dense forests of Africa did not harbor the mosquito that carries malaria, which thrives in sunlight and pools of stagnant water. However, the introduction of horticulture brought great ecological change and fertile breeding grounds to mosquitoes. Land was cleared to plant crops, allowing sunlight to reach the earth. Changes in the soil resulted in standing pools of water conducive to the growth of malaria-carrying mosquitoes. Settled villages grew larger in this abundant new economy, providing the population density that allowed the disease to spread. Thus, we see a connection between culture and biology: cultural adaptations (tools to clear land and horticulture) altered the ecology of the land and allowed malaria-carrying mosquitoes to greatly increase in number, which in turn ultimately led to the increased frequency of the sickle cell allele in the settled population (Relethford 2007). This example also underscores the importance of the holistic perspective in the work of individual anthropologists.

As Erika Bourguignon (1996) points out, although Livingstone was attempting to answer a biological question, it was necessary for him to investigate and understand data from all four fields of anthropology. The distribution of language groups sheds light on migration patterns. Archaeology provided evidence of iron tools used to clear the land. The shift from mobile hunting and gathering to settled agricultural villages yielded an entirely different social structure. Thus, it took all four subdisciplines of anthropology to understand the complexity of sickle cell anemia, its distribution, and why it still exists in many parts of the world.

Anthropology Connects

Anthropologist Marvin Harris has pointed out that anthropologists don't view holism as an end in and of itself; rather, they have embraced the holistic perspective because it is "crucial for solving major riddles of human existence" (1997:25). James Peacock (1988) recounts a tale that exemplifies the pitfalls of looking too closely at the parts and not the whole: a factory worker, at the end of each day, would leave the gate pushing a wheelbarrow. Each day, the guard at the gate would stop the worker, check to make sure the wheelbarrow was empty, and only then allow the worker to exit. Not until several months later was it discovered that the worker had been stealing wheelbarrows. Anthropology's investigation into the wonders of the origins and diverse workings of human life is ongoing, our endeavors in each subdiscipline connected to the other three, always aiming to avoid the factory guard's error of inspecting the contents without regard to the container.

REFERENCES

BERNARD, H. R.
    1980. Personal communication to Patricia Rice.
BONVILLAIN, N.
    1997. *Language, Culture, and Communication: The Meaning of Messages.* Upper Saddle River, NJ: Prentice Hall.
BOURGUIGNON, E.
    1996. "American Anthropology: A Personal View." *General Anthropology* 3(1): 1–7.
ECKHOLM, E.
    2002. "Desire for Sons Drives Use of Prenatal Scans in China." The *New York Times*, June 21.
EHRENREICH, R.
    1996. "Archaeology: Integrating the Sciences and the Humanities." *Anthropology Newsletter*, March 16.
HARRIS, M.
    1997. "Anthropology Needs Holism; Holism Needs Anthropology." In *The Teaching of Anthropology: Problems, Issues, and Decisions,* edited by Conrad Phillip Kottak, Jane J. White, Richard H. Furlow, and Patricia C. Rice, pp. 22–28. Mountain View, CA: Mayfield Publishing Company.

HICKERSON, N. P.

1997. "How to Save Linguistic Anthropology." In *The Teaching of Anthropology: Problems, Issues, and Decisions,* edited by Conrad Phillip Kottak, Jane J. White, Richard H. Furlow, and Patricia C. Rice, pp. 154–164. Mountain View, CA: Mayfield Publishing Company.

JOLLY, C. J. and R. WHITE

1995. *Physical Anthropology and Archaeology.* New York: McGraw-Hill.

KOTTAK, C. P.

2009. *Anthropology: The Exploration of Human Diversity* (13th edition). New York: McGraw-Hill.

NANDA, S. and R. WARMS

2007. *Cultural Anthropology* (9th edition). Belmont, CA: Wadsworth.

PEACOCK, J. L.

1988. *The Anthropological Lens: Harsh Light, Soft Focus.* Cambridge, UK: Cambridge University Press.

RELETHFORD, J. H.

2007. *The Human Species: An Introduction to Biological Anthropology* (7th edition). New York: McGraw-Hill.

SAPIR, E.

1997. (1912) In Bonvillain, N., *Language, Culture, and Communications: The Meaning of Messages.* Upper Saddle River, NJ: Prentice Hall.

SCHULTZ, E. A. and R. H. LAVENDA

2008. *Anthropology: A Perspective on the Human Condition* (7th edition). New York: Oxford University Press.

SCUPIN, R. and C. R. DECORSE

2008. *Anthropology: A Global Perspective* (6th edition). Upper Saddle River, NJ: Prentice Hall.

WILLCOX, D.

1986. *Hmong Folklife.* Marion, NC: Copple House Books.

STUDY QUESTIONS

1. Using the concept of holism and American culture, suggest several themes or areas of culture that anthropologists might investigate.
2. Explain why holism relative to your answer in #1 above might provide more knowledge than the study of single items.

CHAPTER 4

Thinking Theoretically

Philip Carl Salzman
McGill University

What do anthropologists mean when they talk about theories such as cultural materialism, structuralism, or postmodernism (Salzman 2001)? How do these theories relate to what anthropologists study? How exactly do anthropologists, and how exactly can you, think theoretically? And why do they, and why would you, want to think theoretically?

THE PARTICULAR AND THE GENERAL

Anthropologists in their ethnographic field research on particular cultures look for patterns of thought, belief, activity, organization, and behavior (See Chapter 2). When patterns are identified, they are sometimes called customs, norms, institutions, worldviews, or structures. Particular patterns can be identified with a specific time and place, such as the Trobriand Islands in the second decade of the twentieth century, Nuerland in the 1930s, Tikopia in the 1930s, Baluchistan in the 1960s and 1970s, or highland Sardinia in the 1990s. A. R. Radcliffe-Brown (1952:1), an originator of British social anthropology, called patterns found in a particular place and time *idiographic* because they are unique and specific to those times and places. Another term that could be used for these specific patterns is *descriptive*. By this we mean that the pattern discussed is close to the facts at a low *level of abstraction* from the particulars of a time and place.

But anthropologists are also interested in theory, which is general rather than particular, at a high rather than low level of abstraction. Theory is far from the facts of a specific time and place because it is intended to encompass a wide range of various specifics. Radcliffe-Brown (1952:1) called the quest for general knowledge **nomothetic** (meaning "law giving"), to distinguish it from the search for idiographic

26

facts. Most anthropologists today would just call general formulations **theory**. The main point is that facts tied to particular times and places are specific, whereas theory is general and encompasses many facts from many times and places.

HEURISTIC THEORIES

The most general theories I call **heuristic theories**, which means theories that guide our inquiries. Heuristic theories are very general in the sense that they are very abstract and purport to cover myriad facts from many times and places. Robert Merton (1957:9) describes such theories as "general orientations toward data, suggesting types of variables [factors that can vary, such as type of religion or marriage practices] that need somehow to be taken into account, rather than clear, verifiable statements of relationships between specified variables."

The dominant heuristic theory in the first half of the twentieth century was **functionalism**. In the functionalist perspective, society was understood as having a number of distinct parts, such as the institutions of politics, religion, and economics, that were interconnected with one another and mutually influential. In the functionalist perspective, any particular custom, rule, activity, or practice could be understood in relation to the other parts of the society in terms of its function for the other parts and the whole of society. For example, ancestor cults, praying to and leaving offerings for dead ancestors, were seen as an ideological support and rationale for lineage group organization in which all group members are descended from common ancestors (Colson 1962; Chapter 1). In this case, the "distinct parts" that influence each other are religion (ancestor cults) and social organization (lineages). Another related example is the functionalist argument that kinship terminologies and norms for relationships between kin, such as whether the relationships are strict and authoritative or warm and supportive, reflect group organization, with relations between seniors and juniors in the same descent group being strict and authoritative and those in different descent groups being warm and supportive (Radcliffe-Brown 1952; Chapter 2).

Thus functionalism offered a vision of the world and how it works and so directed anthropologists to focus their research on the elements and relations identified by the theory. Anthropologists under the influence of functionalism were guided in their ethnographic field research to search for functional interconnections between customs, practices, and institutions. In their analyses, functionalist anthropologists explained customs, rules, and activities by their functions, by the effects of specific practices, beliefs, and norms on other institutions and practices, or by their effects on the continuity and existence of the society as a whole.

Heuristic theories guide anthropological thought by offering a vision of social and cultural reality and directing attention to what it deems is important. Each heuristic theory proposes a way of looking at the world, a way of carrying out research, and a way of understanding research findings. Functionalism did that for the first half of the twentieth century, and many anthropologists continue to be influenced by functionalist heuristics in their research.

Let us examine a more recent heuristic theory. *Cultural materialism* (Harris 1979) draws on the broad stream of Marxist materialism but adds an anthropological flavor. The main principle of cultural materialism is called infrastructural determinism (Harris 1979:56) and is expressed this way:

> The etic behavioral modes of production and reproduction probabilistically determine the etic behavioral domestic and political economy, which in turn probabilistically determine the behavioral and mental emic structures. (Harris 1979:55–56)

This means that (1) the infrastructure, how people make a living and reproduce, shapes (2) the structure, how people organize themselves, and how they organize themselves shapes (3) the superstructure, people's ideas and such activities as ritual, art, and sports. Harris (1979:26–27) says explicitly that cultural materialism is a "research strategy"—in our terms, a heuristic theory—to guide research. But its goal is very ambitious:

> The aim of cultural materialism in particular is to account for the origin, maintenance, and change of the global inventory of socio-cultural differences and similarities. (Harris 1979:27)

In this sense, cultural materialism is a heuristic theory *par excellence.* It should explain everything!

How would cultural materialism guide an anthropologist's thoughts and research? First, the anthropologist would want to be sure to collect information on the infrastructure, structure, and superstructure in order to see the relations between them. Second, the anthropologist would want to know clearly what information or data collected is **etic**, based on observation on people's activities, and which information is **emic**, based on people's ideas. Third, the anthropologist would seek explanation for any particular custom, practice, or belief in the infrastructure, that is, technology of subsistence, technoenvironmental relations, work patterns, mating patterns, or demography.

An example of cultural materialism is Harris's (1966, 1974) examination of sacred cattle in India. Harris wants to know why "clean caste" Hindus of India believe that cows are sacred and that cows must not be killed and their meat must not be eaten. There are tens of millions of cows in India, but they are not slaughtered, and their meat is forbidden to Hindus. Surely plenty of Indians could use the nourishment, so why do they abstain?

Harris's first answer is that Hindus abstain from eating beef because it is sacred. The cultural rule that forbids Hindus to eat beef is very important because it overrules immediate individual needs and thus serves the long-term needs of the collectivity. Harris's second answer is that Indian cattle are a critical contributor to the vegetarian diet of caste Hindus. Unlike beef, the milk and butter oil (ghee) that cattle contribute to the Indian diet are renewable. Cow dung serves as fertilizer for the grain fields and for fuel. And cattle pull the plows for grain cultivation.

Because the grain, milk, and vegetable diet of Hindus is very efficiently produced, it can support the large Indian population. In contrast, enough meat could be produced to support only a small percentage of the Indian population. In short, Indian cattle are thought to be sacred because they must be protected to make their contribution to the efficient Hindu vegetarian diet. Here Harris is arguing that the explanation for a religious belief is found in the way people make a living.

Heuristic theories such as functionalism and cultural materialism provide the anthropologist with a general approach to the world and to research and offer guidelines for thinking about and commenting on research findings. Because heuristic theories are so general, they cannot be disproved in themselves. There is no one finding that can show that a heuristic theory is wrong. If a functional relationship is not found, a functionalist critic could say that the researcher did not look hard enough. If in a cultural materialist analysis, infrastructural determination cannot be found, Harris would say that the determination is probabilistic and exists in most cases if not in this exception. So heuristic theories cannot really be tested to see whether they are true or false but instead are generally judged to be useful or not useful, fruitful or not fruitful in generating interesting results.

SUBSTANTIVE THEORIES

A second kind of theory we can call **substantive theories** in that they specify a definite relationship between two or more sets or categories of social and cultural phenomena. They are more specific and particular than heuristic theories, but they are more general than descriptions tied to particular times and places. Robert Merton (1957:9) called these theories **middle-range theories** because they are less abstract than grand or heuristic theories but more abstract than descriptions of particular cases. Thus it is easier to bring data or evidence to bear on these theories to test whether they hold up in the face of descriptive, ethnographic case material. Substantive or middle-range theories therefore can be judged in a more definitive fashion as to whether they are correct.

As an example, let us examine Julian Steward's (1963; Chapter 7) theory of the patrilineal band. Steward was studying hunters and gatherers. He found that some are **patrilineal** and **patrilocal**; that is, as a group they are constituted as descendants of a common ancestor in the male line, and when the men marry they stay at home, but women who marry outside the group go to live with their husbands. The patrilineal hunting band differs from other hunters who lived as independent families or whose bands were composite, with no unity based on common descent, and with men and women coming from other groups and going to other groups. Steward asked what explains the presence of the patrilineal hunting band rather than separate families or composite bands.

Drawing on his knowledge of many different hunting groups, Steward formulated a theory that specified exactly the conditions in which patrilineal bands would be found. He argues, having cited case material from the Bushmen of southern Africa, central African Negritos, Semang from Malaya, Philippine

Negritos, and Australian Aborigines, that four factors produce the patrilineal band (1963:135):

1. A population density of one person or less—usually much less—per square mile, which is caused by a hunting and gathering technology in areas of scarce wild foods;
2. An environment in which the principal food is game that is nonmigratory and scattered, which makes it advantageous for men to remain in the general territory of their birth;
3. Transportation restricted to human carriers;
4. The cultural–psychological fact, which cannot be explained by local adaptation, that groups of kin who associate together intimately tend to extend incest taboos from the biological family to the extended family, thus requiring group exogamy.

Note that although the relationship between the form to be explained, the patrilineal band and the four conditions underlying it is specified in a definite fashion, the theory is somewhat abstract, dealing with categories of phenomena—patrilineal bands and four conditions—rather than one unique case limited in space and time. The definiteness of the relationship specified allows us to test the theory. By looking at some other cases of hunting groups, such as the Inuit (Eskimo) of arctic America or the Kwakiutl of the northwest coast of North America, we can check to see whether the relationship specified by Steward holds up. If we were to find a patrilineal hunting group that depended on migratory game rather than on nonmigratory and scattered game (Steward's third condition) or a nonpatrilineal composite band that seems to fulfill Steward's four conditions, we would throw serious doubt on Steward's theory.

Substantive or middle-range theories can be inspired by heuristic theories. This is what Harris intended in formulating his cultural materialist research strategy:

> Cultural materialism shares with other scientific strategies an epistemology which seeks to restrict fields of inquiry to events, entities, and relationships that are knowable by means of explicit, logico-empirical, inductive-deductive, quantifiable public procedures or "operations" subject to replication by independent observers. (1979:27)

Harris's "explicit, logico-empirical, inductive–deductive, quantifiable public procedures" are the testing of substantive, middle-range theories.

Not all heuristic theories lead to or are consistent with explicit, substantive, middle-range theories. The reason for this is that not all heuristic theories are consistent with a scientific approach to studying society and culture. Science aims at explanation, the identification of causal relationships, which requires substantive or middle-range theories. In contrast, some anthropological heuristic theories

are more oriented to the humanities and advocate **explication** rather than explanation. Explication usually involves exploring the meaning that ideas and actions
and patterns and practices have for the people involved. Explication thus tends to
focus on elaboration of the specific and particular rather than attempting to
relate causal factors in middle-range theories.

The most influential humanistic heuristic theory is *interpretationalism*,
invented almost single-handedly by Clifford Geertz and first elucidated in *The
Interpretation of Cultures* (1973). His focus is on meaning:

> The concept of culture I espouse . . . is essentially a semiotic one. Believing, with
> Max Weber, that man is an animal suspended in webs of significance he himself has
> spun, I take culture to be those webs, and the analysis of it to be therefore not an exper-
> imental science in search of law but an interpretive one in search of meaning. It is expli-
> cation I am after, construing social expressions on their surface enigmatical. (1973:5)

By saying that he is not in search of "law," Geertz is saying that he is not trying to
find scientific laws or substantive theories to explain human life. Geertz elaborates:

> As interworked systems of construable signs (. . . symbols), culture is not a power,
> something to which social events, behaviors, institutions, or processes can be causally
> attributed; it is a context, something within which they can be intelligibly—that is,
> thickly—described. (1973:14)

Geertz's alternative to substantive, middle-range theory is "thick description," an elaborate account of the many meanings involved in any specific human
activity in any particular time and place. So, for Geertz, there is heuristic theory as
a guide and thick description, with no substantive theory in between.

Partly under the influence of Geertz and interpretive anthropology, a more
recent heuristic theory, *postmodernism* (Marcus and Fischer 1986; Clifford and
Marcus 1986; Marcus 1998), rejects a scientific approach and all **empiricism** and
positivism in anthropology as false and politically suspect, and rejects any "master
narrative" as one-sided. Postmodernism stresses the subjectivity of the researcher
and the injustice in treating the subjects of research, the people being studied, as
objects. Rejecting any formulation of scientific, substantive, middle-range theories, postmodernism has stressed giving "voice" to the subjects of research so that
they can tell their own stories rather than have our theories or interpretations
imposed on them. So postmodernism too goes directly from heuristic theory to
"voice," with no intermediate theoretical formulation.

THEORIES IN PALEOANTHROPOLOGY

Archaeologists, who study people's culture in the past, are closer to cultural
anthropologists in terms of their use of theories than biological anthropologists
because they share culture as their central focus, and it is theories that help us
explain culture, thus tying the two anthropological subfields. Additionally,

American archaeologists, brought up in the New World intellectual tradition that claims "archaeology is anthropology," would make only one change in this essay to be compatible with their own concepts of theory: they would put everything in the past tense because they focus on people's culture in the past. They would agree there are heuristic theories, and many still ascribe to functionalism to see how cultures in the past worked. Others are materialists, to some extent because the nature of their data is material culture and they often "force" material items to tell stories even larger than the items themselves. But they would add a third heuristic theory, called ecoculturalism, which is also a guide to archaeological inquiries because within the long time frame in which archaeologists work, climate changes. All anthropologists, particularly ecoculturalists, firmly believe cultures exist in an environmental context, and if the climate changes, so will the culture. Ecoculturalism therefore is often used by archaeologists as a causal explanation for change. By contrast, cultural anthropologists do not normally study groups long enough to use environmental change as causal.

Particularly since 1960, archaeologists under the banner of Lewis Binford (1972, 1977) have embraced middle-range theory to attempt to explain why cultures were the way they were in the past. They focus on experiments and analysis of topics not tied to a particular time or place to see whether their assumptions are supported. For example, in the 1950s Russian archaeologist Sergei Semenov (1964), working alone in St. Petersburg, discovered the principles of microwear analysis in an attempt to explain the function of prehistoric flint tools. He used artifacts in the collections at St. Petersburg that were obviously mostly from prehistoric Russian times. Would these principles be applicable to microwear on tools in prehistoric France or prehistoric Africa? Middle-range theory tested this idea through comparisons of collections and through "blind tests" in which one experimenter made and used a number of different kinds of tools, leaving different kinds of microwear on them, and the second experimenter looked at the tools (after they had been washed to make sure no clues were left behind) and their microwear and came to conclusions as to their function (Keeley and Newcomer 1977). Postmodernism has its advocates in archaeology as well, but although postmodern archaeologists criticize other theoretical positions and reject all scientific procedures and **logical positivism** (See Chapter 7), they have not produced work that has advanced our understanding of the past.

Biological anthropologists, by contrast, listen to a different theoretical drummer. With few exceptions, biological anthropologists are Darwinian scientists. That means that as they attempt to understand human evolution and the state of modern humans today, they do so under the strict guidance of Darwinian principles. They ask, how did natural selection favor bipedalism? Why were brains late in becoming larger? Why do people who live around the equator today have darker skins than those who live further away? One of Darwin's tenets in evolution was that regardless of cause (most of which he did not understand in 1850), because of millions of years of evolution, populations were at any time well adapted to their environments. So to what was bipedalism adapted? Why did change from four-leggedness to two-leggedness better adapt hominids (prehumans) to their environment?

Although biological anthropologists study humans just as archaeologists and cultural anthropologists do, one of the big differences between them is in their explanatory theories. Biological anthropologists adhere to one theory, natural selection, which, if Darwin was correct, yields adaptation. By contrast, cultural anthropologists choose from among several kinds of theories to guide them in finding explanations. Nonetheless, all anthropologists, no matter what their specialization, think theoretically because it guides what they see and how they interpret what they see to explain the human condition.

HOW CAN YOU THINK THEORETICALLY?

Whenever we think about things or look at things, we are guided by a heuristic theory. That theory may be an implicit one based on "American culture" and be considered "common sense," or it may be an explicit one based on our religion or our political position, or it may be an explicit one based in an academic discipline such as anthropology, economics, history, or literary criticism. What we assume is important; what we look for, what we expect to find, and the very categories and their labels are based on our heuristic theories. (See Chapter 7 for a discussion of biases, assumptions, and preconceptions in research.)

One important step in thinking theoretically is being aware of our heuristics, making explicit our guiding theory, and giving attention to its assumptions and implications. In other words, part of thinking theoretically is bringing heuristic theory into our consciousness and taking a critical stance to it. By being aware of our own heuristic theories, we are able to proceed in a more self-critical and intellectually more responsible fashion.

Another step in thinking theoretically is being aware that any account, anthropological or other, of society or culture is based on heuristic theory, whether or not that is made explicit. Let's say we are reading a book on mortuary ritual in Melanesia that seems pretty descriptive (maybe too descriptive for our taste). But even if the author is not explicit about the heuristic approach, the author's treatment of mortuary ritual will reflect the author's heuristic theory. So we have to ask ourselves, "What is the guiding heuristic theory?" For example, if the author is a cultural materialist, there will be an attempt to explain mortuary ritual (which would be regarded as superstructure) in terms of forms of social organization (structure) or the way people make a living (infrastructure). But if the author is an interpretive anthropologist, mortuary ritual would be explicated in terms of the wider realms of meaning, such as the people's metaphysics (for example, their ideas about the continuing influence of dead ancestors or about an afterlife or rebirth), theology (for example, ideas about gods or God, about final judgment), and social assumptions (for example, whether social rank continues after death). Thinking theoretically means knowing the theoretical background of the various accounts and reports and commentaries offered by anthropologists or anyone else.

The third step in thinking theoretically is explicitly relating your own work, in writing papers or writing exams, to your theoretical assumptions and framework and to the theoretical frameworks, both heuristic and substantive, important in anthropology or other relevant fields. In other words, however much you are focused on reporting facts, you must relate these to the theories of the authors and to the other theories prevalent in anthropology. So it is necessary to be familiar with the theories and to be able to see when they underlay or influence the discussion and to be able to explain this as part of your own presentations.

Finally, thinking theoretically means working with theory, whether heuristic or substantive, in your own thinking and presentations. Other people's theoretical formulations, even those of illustrious anthropologists, are not the final word, but can be used as bases on which to develop and elaborate theoretical ideas. Let me give a simple example from my own thinking when I was a student. Merton (1957) spoke about manifest and latent functions of customs and institutions: manifest functions were desired and recognized consequences, whereas latent functions were undesired and unrecognized consequences. If sexual freedom was a manifest function of the sexual revolution of the 1960s, children being born to single, teenage mothers is a latent function of the sexual revolution. But it occurred to me that some consequences could also be desired but unrecognized, such as (this may or may not be true) children's increased intellectual power resulting from watching television, or could be undesired but recognized, such as sending kids to school reducing parental authority and control. Although this little conceptual innovation was no great sociological breakthrough, and I gained no great fame from it, my teachers were a little bit impressed. Most important, it helped me along the road to thinking theoretically.

REFERENCES

BINFORD, L. R.
   1972. *An Archaeological Perspective.* New York: Seminar Press.
   1977. *For Theory Building in Archaeology.* Orlando, FL: Academic Press.
CLIFFORD, J. and G. E. MARCUS, eds.
   1986. *Writing Culture: The Poetics and Politics of Ethnography.* Berkeley, CA: University of California Press.
COLSON, E.
   1962. *The Plateau Tonga of Northern Rhodesia.* Manchester, UK: Manchester University Press.
GEERTZ, C.
   1973. *The Interpretation of Cultures.* New York: Basic Books.
HARRIS, M.
   1966. "The Cultural Ecology of India's Sacred Cattle." *Current Anthropology* 7: 51–66.
   1974. *Cows, Pigs, Wars, and Witches: The Riddles of Culture.* New York: Random House.
   1979. *Cultural Materialism.* New York: Random House.
KEELEY, L. and M. NEWCOMER
   1977. "Microwear Analysis of Experimental Flint Tools: A Test Case." *Journal of Archaeological Science* 4: 29–62.

MARCUS, G. E.
1998. *Ethnography through Thick and Thin.* Princeton, NJ: Princeton University Press.
MARCUS, G. E. and M. J. FISCHER, eds.
1986. *Anthropology and Cultural Critique: An Experimental Moment in the Human Sciences.* Chicago, IL: University of Chicago Press.
MERTON, R.
1957. *Social Theory and Social Structure.* Glencoe, IL: Free Press.
RADCLIFFE-BROWN, A. R.
1952. *Structure and Function in Primitive Society.* London, UK: Cohen and West.
SALZMAN, P. C.
2001. *Understanding Culture: An Introduction to Anthropological Theory.* Prospect Heights, IL: Waveland.
SEMENOV, S. A.
1964. *Prehistoric Technology.* New York: Barnes & Noble.
STEWARD, J.
1963. *Theory of Culture Change.* Urbana, IL: University of Illinois Press.

STUDY QUESTIONS

1. As stated in the first question asked in this chapter, why will thinking theoretically help you think anthropologically?
2. You are going to highland New Guinea to study a neighborhood's culture. Pick the heuristic theory that you find the most interesting and discuss how you would use it to approach studying that culture.

CHAPTER 5

Using Science to Think Anthropologically[1]

Robin O'Brian

Elmira College

Patricia C. Rice

West Virginia University

Geoff Clark, a well-known expert on the Spanish Upper Paleolithic period, said to one of us recently, "I am a scientist first, an anthropologist second, and an archaeologist third." By using this order, he is stating that he thinks like a scientist first (method), like an anthropologist second (broad-based content), and like an archaeologist last (specific content). No matter what our specialization in anthropology, we must first and foremost think scientifically, and as a student of anthropology, you must think scientifically too. How do we do this, and just as pertinent, how should you do this?

Science is a way of thinking about something. It is a method of seeking knowledge. It does not necessarily involve bubbling retorts or white lab coats. Because scientists believe there is an orderly world out there where events (past or present) can be explained if adequate observation or data are used properly, that world can be known. And it is **knowledge** that scientists are searching for. Science goes beyond data gathering and description in order to explain things and happenings.

For example, *biological anthropologists* do not just excavate and then describe fossils of our ancestors; they attempt to explain why there has been change between then and now, and if there is a large enough sample, why one fossil looks different from one that is of the same age. *Archaeologists* don't just describe the flint tools or ceramic shards they excavate; they try to explain how those tools were used. And although it seems quite different, other anthropologists use what people do and say as the data they examine. A *cultural anthropologist* doing research in rural India might note that there is a widespread presence of cattle even in areas of malnutrition and wonder why people do not eat beef (Harris 1966). A specialist in **linguistics** in the same neighborhood would note the symbols for sounds in the language spoken by the people and then attempt to figure out how they can engage in trade with people in a neighboring group who speak a totally different language.

Scientists do not have to use statistics or do experiments to do science. All they have to do is to think scientifically. To think scientifically is to do science, and doing science concerns its method. What scientists use is the **scientific method**. The scientific method begins with something worth investigating, some question for which we do not have an answer. If there is a question, there is probably more than one possible answer to it. When the question is stated with a possible answer, it becomes a **hypothesis**. Put another way, a hypothesis is a good guess about something. Here are some anthropological examples. "I hypothesize that modern humans were on Earth about 100,000 years ago." This is a good guess based on existing fossil finds and modern dating techniques. "He hypothesized that many more tools could be made from a flint nodule if the flint knapper made blades instead of flakes." This is a good guess based on previous flint knapping experiments by a flint knapper. (Note: Flint knapping in prehistoric times was the method our ancestors used to make usable tools; in modern times, flint knapping is done experimentally by archaeologists to try to decide how tools may have been made and used in the past by observing marks on prehistoric tools.) "I hypothesize that Indian farmers don't eat their cattle because they are more useful as plow animals, and if they eat them they won't be able to farm." This is a good guess based on observation and talking with the farmers. Finally, "I hypothesize that people in the New Guinea highlands can trade with neighbors who do not speak their language because what they are trading is very valuable to them, and they are able to do the actual trade through gestures." This is a good guess based again on observation (the gestures) and talking to the people involved.

Whichever hypothesis you want to follow through on, the fossil, the artifact, the customs, or the language, the next step is to attempt to discover whether it is false or supported. Many interesting things cannot be falsified and therefore are not subject to scientific investigation. Some of us would like to know whether the tooth fairy exists, but hypothesizing that it does exist (or does not) is not scientific because the hypothesis cannot be falsified.

To **test** any of these hypotheses, the scientist–anthropologist would have to gather data pertinent to the question asked to falsify or support it. You can't gather and use data on penguins to answer a question about human burial rituals. The fossils, artifacts, observations on customs, and tape recordings of specific spoken languages are all considered **evidence** or **data** and are used to support or falsify a particular hypothesis. If the evidence supports it, the hypothesis is supported; if not, it is falsified.

What do we mean by evidence or data supporting or falsifying any hypothesis? For the hypothesis suggesting modern humans had evolved by 100,000 years ago, if a bioanthropologist finds a new complete fossil in Ethiopia that was securely dated at 140,000 years ago and showed traits that were 98 percent the same as contemporary humans, the hypothesis about the date of the first modern humans would be supported. If, however, that well-dated fossil showed numerous traits that linked it closer to previous species in our lineage, the hypothesis would be falsified, that is, not supported. To take one more example, if a modern male flint knapper could make twice as many useable blades as flakes from the same size flint nodule, the hypothesis that claimed people changed their tool making because they could make more tools with the same amount of flint would be supported. But if a modern female flint knapper made fewer blades than flakes, the hypothesis would be falsified. We do not know if only one sex of our ancestors made tools but can assume that males have always had more upper arm strength than women. As the leading philosopher of science, Karl Popper, said many years ago, if a hypothesis cannot be falsified, it isn't science. We would add that if a hypothesis is falsified, it is "back to the drawing board."

Testing hypotheses is not the solitary job of a single scientist testing and retesting his or her own work. Other scientists may take a skeptical position and retest the hypothesis to see whether they get the same results. If the same data and methods are used, *replication* can support or refute the hypothesis. Thus, science is a collective rather than an individual enterprise.

Hypotheses can be found to be false, but they *cannot be proved* because all of the data pertinent to answering the question are never available. We do not have the remains of all of the people who were alive 100,000 years ago, we do not have all of the flint blades and flakes ever made, we were not in India or New Guinea when most of their social customs originated, and we cannot watch every trading expedition. Scientists never use the terms **"proof"** or "prove" because such terms imply certainty. The same is true of the word **"truth"** because it implies certainty beyond a shadow of a doubt. Scientists know better than to claim they search for truth because it is unattainable. They are content with finding knowledge, defined as a description of something that is probably correct, given the available data. But if truth and proof are finite and nonchanging, knowledge is changeable and fluid. Today's knowledge is yesterday's antiquated myth, and tomorrow's knowledge will show that half of what we think we know now is wrong. Scientists look for change in knowledge, and it is healthy to be skeptical about one's own work as well as that of others.

Some change in knowledge is slow in coming; some is very fast. As an example of slow change in knowledge, consider how biological traits are transmitted from one generation to another. For thousands of years, people have certainly noticed that children look more like their parents than they look like strangers. Until the end of the 1800s, scientists thought traits were carried in the blood; then Gregor Mendel devised his Laws of Inheritance, with 34 years elapsing until his ideas became known and accepted. Finally, it was another 50 years before we could speak of the beginning of modern genetics in the 1950s.

Other changes in knowledge are remarkably speedy, such as the discovery of Ötzi, the Ice Man, a mummy found on the Austrian–Italian border in the Alps in 1991. When first discovered, it was thought to be a casualty of a previous year's bad storm, but the condition of the body tissue suggested it was old. At first, it was dated as perhaps 2,000 years old, but more recently, carbon 14 dated the mummy at 5,300 years ago. As to the cause of his death, early knowledge suggested that he froze to death, and then the ice and snow desiccated his tissue, mummifying it. Very recently, a computed axial tomography (CAT) scan discovered an arrow in his shoulder, and it is now believed that this caused his death, directly or indirectly (Bahn 2002; Fowler 2000). At any point in the past decade, our knowledge about the Ice Man was based on the data we had at that time, but as additional evidence became available, our knowledge changed. And it will continue to change. It is a good thing that none of the scientists involved claimed to have "proved" anything!

There are two variations of the scientific method in terms of the order of steps taken to go from interesting findings to conclusions. If a hypothesis is generated about something interesting before any data are gathered (observations made, people talked to, languages heard), the type of science is called **deductive science**. That hypothesis could have come from someone else's previous work that the particular scientist did not agree with, or it could have come from a brainstorming session with other scientists over a beer at the end of a day, or it could have come in a dream. The point is that it is a good guess about something, as in "I bet they can trade with their neighbors through gesture even if they can't understand each other." In deductive science, the scientist then gathers appropriate data to see whether the data support that guess. If they do, it is supported; if not, it was a bad guess. The other variation is called **inductive science**. In inductive methods, data about a particular subject of interest are freely gathered, with no preconceived idea of whether they will answer any question or how they would answer any question. Out of the data gathering and analysis comes a tentative conclusion about that subject, and that conclusion becomes the hypothesis. Now different data must be gathered to test the hypothesis for support or falsification. So, regardless of where in the process one begins, the process is the same: hypothesis, data gathering, data analysis, conclusions.

Here are three examples of inductively and deductively generated research projects:

(1) Everyone "knows" that 25,000-year-old **Venus statuettes** from the European Upper Paleolithic period and carved from ivory, bone, or precious stone were fertility dolls. Right? Not necessarily. A female anthropologist wondered whether the anthropologists who had studied Venus statuettes previously— all male—were biased by the obvious nakedness of the statuettes and attributed fertility to them because of it. She decided to look at every one of the 180 Venuses and assess each relative to its age (did the artist attempt to sculpt a young, middle-aged, or old woman?) and state of pregnancy (did the artist attempt to sculpt a pregnant woman?). After categorizing every possible Venus, the result was that

only 17 percent of the statuettes were both in the right age category and obviously pregnant. Not only did this suggest that the fertility doll idea was incorrect, but the conclusions also led to a new hypothesis: women were sculpted because they provided most of the food eaten by the group, did become pregnant and have babies, and were the important focus of house and home (Rice 1981). New evidence was then gathered to support (or not) the new hypothesis. You should recognize this as *inductive* research because data were freely gathered, resulting in a hypothesis. The research also suggests that male and female scientists observe the same things—in this case, Venus statuettes—differently just because they are of different sexes. (See Chapter 7 for more examples of why scientists disagree.)

(2) A specialist in prehistoric art published research that concluded that a painting on the ceiling in the famous 18,000-year-old Altamira cave was a bison, not a wild boar, as previous experts believed. Another specialist in prehistoric art in turn questioned the bison identification of the animal and set out to find data to support the hypothesis that it was a boar after all. This specialist measured various points on the animals in question, other bison and boars in cave art and live bison and boars, and came up with four ratios that described the shape of the two animals (relative leg length and body shape). By comparing the ratios of all of the animals, the specialist found that the animal in question matched the boar, not the bison (Rice 1992). You should recognize this as *deductive* research because the researcher had already generated the hypothesis ("It is a boar") before collecting any data (the ratios).

(3) If you wonder whether Maya women become farmers because there is increasing economic need where they live and decide to test this hypothesis by conducting research in southern Mexico, this is deductive science because your hypothesis, "Rural Maya women will enter farming because of economic need," precedes your trip to Mexico. You have already predicted a reason for the Maya women to become farmers. But when you arrive and discover that indeed there is economic need but that women are becoming commercial weavers, not farmers, your hypothesis is disproved or falsified. So, like any good researcher, you collect a lot of data about women weavers. You ask them about where they live, what they weave, and how they learned to weave, and about their friends, communities, religions, and families. This is inductive science because the data were gathered freely, with no assumed question asked. Although this sounds a good deal like plain conversation, and it is, it is also more evidence for other questions you might ask. When you return from your fieldwork and analyze your evidence, if you discover that those Maya women who live in urban settings and are Protestant converts don't know how to weave and sell commercially made crafts, whereas rural women who still learn weaving from their mothers sell traditional handwoven crafts, this becomes an inductive hypothesis ("Protestant women are less likely than Catholic women to know and use traditional weaving skills") that arose after you collected your data (O'Brian 1994). You would probably return to collect new data, perhaps quantitative, to support or reject that hypothesis and then perhaps move into some of the "why" questions. Research generates further research.

The word hypothesis has another scientific meaning related to the *level of confidence* a scientist has about the results of an investigation. If a scientist has a medium amount of confidence in a conclusion, perhaps because he or she did the actual work, the phrase "the hypothesis is supported" is appropriate. If that hypothesis is tested and retested by many different scientists over a period of years and it is still supported (not rejected or found to be false), its level of confidence raises it to the level of a **theory**. When a theory has been around for a hundred years or more and hundreds of scientists have tried to disprove it with no luck, its level of confidence is extremely high, and we call it a **law**. Any one of these—hypothesis, theory, or law—can still be found to be false, but the higher the confidence level, the less likely it is to be found false. (See Chapter 4 for other meanings of "theory.")

For example, when Charles Darwin came up with the idea of natural selection, it was a hypothesis. It explained some observable things in nature, such as the shape of tortoise shells in the Gálapagos Islands, but there was a lot about nature that was still unknown, such as genetics. By the turn of the twentieth century, scientists knew about mutations and some genetic principles, and more of the biological world could be explained by natural selection. At this point, natural selection became a theory because the original hypothesis had gained in its level of confidence. It has now been 150 years since the *Origin of Species* was published, with thousands of scientists attempting to disprove natural selection. It has been tweaked and changed in places, but in general, Darwin's version of natural selection has not changed. Our level of confidence in it gives it law-like status. Thus hypothesis, theory, and law are places on a continuum of scientific confidence. Not much knowledge is law-like, the term "theory" tends to be overused, and thus most of what knowledge we have is in the form of hypotheses, ready to move to a higher level of confidence if merited, or tested yet again to see whether it remains supported.

An example of a hypothesis in the bioarchaeological world of anthropology that is still being tested and retested concerns the role of Neandertal in modern human ancestry. The hypothesis could be stated either way: Neandertals were in our ancestry or they were not. A more fully developed hypothesis might be, "Neandertals were a separate species from *Homo sapiens* in Europe even though the two groups overlapped, in Western Europe at least, for perhaps 10,000 years." Some experts have tested the hypothesis by comparing fossils of the two populations, concluding that they differ in enough traits to call them different species and that they were not in our ancestry at all; some have tested it using mitochondrial DNA (mtDNA) on four Neandertals, several early modern humans, and contemporary humans, concluding that there are too many genetic differences for them to be a single species. These tests supported the hypothesis. Other experts suggest that mtDNA is very susceptible to contamination by modern humans and that, even if it isn't, we really do not know how much difference there would have to be between human populations for interbreeding to be impossible. This lack of knowledge is because there is no other species close enough to modern humans to test for successful or unsuccessful interbreeding. But other experts point to a number of biological traits occurring in the vast majority of Neandertal fossils and subsequently in modern human invaders and claim that those traits must have come about through interbreeding of the two populations. This rejects the hypothesis. (See Chapter 7 for further insights into this problem.) The point here is that scientists keep testing and retesting hypotheses, and in some cases, new research supports and in some cases it rejects the original hypothesis. Sometimes falsification removes the hypothesis from further study, whereas in the case of the Neandertal hypothesis, sides are so entrenched that the testing on both sides will continue.

A cultural example of testing and retesting refers to how people rear and understand children and teenagers, something that is of fundamental interest to most people. In the 1920s, Margaret Mead hypothesized that raising children in the traditional Polynesian society of Samoa would produce relaxed, easygoing teenagers. She suggested that they differed dramatically from American teenagers, who seemed full of emotional turmoil. Mead concluded that the seeming difference between Samoan and American teenagers meant that adolescence was strongly shaped by culture, not biology (Mead 1928).

Much later, in the 1980s, another anthropologist, Derek Freeman, using data he had collected from elsewhere in Samoa in the 1940s, argued that Samoan teenagers had a good deal of anxiety and turmoil, although they expressed it differently from Americans. He argued that, contrary to Mead, adolescence probably was a biological state experienced by teenagers in all cultures (Freeman 1983). Freeman's work has been criticized by other anthropologists wanting to test his hypothesis. It appears that Mead and Freeman both were a little bit right and a little bit wrong and that at least some adolescent moodiness is biologically driven but that culture, the rules and ideas of a given society, shapes the way teenagers behave and express their emotions. The issue is not closed, and other cultural anthropologists will continue to test the biological and cultural hypotheses with data from groups they have studied.

What do scientists mean when they speak or write of data or evidence? How do they get it? What do they do with it? Chapter 10 focuses exclusively on doing anthropological research, and Chapter 13 focuses on doing fieldwork. We will therefore be brief in discussing how anthropologists go about getting and analyzing data or evidence. Anthropological data or evidence varies by subdiscipline. To a biological anthropologist, the data may come from excavating fossils, analyzing fossils found by others, or work on modern people. Some biological anthropologists, such as Meave Leakey, Alan Walker, or Don Johanson purposely look for fossils in our human lineage, Meave Leakey and Alan Walker at sites in Kenya looking for fossils that are in the neighborhood of 3 to 1 million years ago and Don Johanson in Ethiopia looking for fossils several million years older than this. Other biological anthropologists compare single anatomical features through time, such as evidence of bipedalism or brain capacities.

Archaeologists often use physical **artifacts** such as tools as their data or evidence, but they can also use ecofacts such as pollen to indicate prehistoric diet or environmental context. Although tools are important because they tell archaeologists what people did for a living, often the nature of trade, and sometimes even social organization, other artifacts tell us even more: a bit of twine embossed in a chunk of clay tells us that 24,000 years ago, people were making twine and probably weaving cloth or making nets for fishing. Grains stuck in fired pottery can tell us what crops might have been domesticated. **Cave paintings** going back as early as 32,000 years and Venus figurines may tell us about social organization and the relative rank of the sexes in Paleolithic times (Rice and Paterson 1988). Finally, the finding of burials, shrines, or statuary may give us a glimpse of people's religion in prehistoric times. By definition, an artifact is any remains of something made by a human in the past, such as a tool, a cave painting, or a burial. The artifacts normally don't "speak for themselves," and have to be interpreted, but they are evidence nonetheless.

Culturally, evidence includes the tools modern people use, but it can also be people's behavior, their conversations and ideas, and their traditions and customs. For example, if an ethnographer visits people in a lowland Amazonian village and writes down whatever he observes them doing when he arrives and does this many times over the course of a number of months, he can discover, statistically, how people spend their days. Although the people may tell the ethnographer one thing—that men work harder than women, for example—the data from all of those visits might show that women work more because when families sit around and talk after a meal, women also busy themselves with tasks while men and children do not. Indeed, Allen Johnson (1975), working among the Machiguenga in Peru, found exactly that and showed how his careful collection of time allocation data provided results that surprised even him.

In this cultural example, all the simple things that people do in their daily lives have been transformed into evidence, and understanding its larger meaning depends on how the anthropologist collects and analyzes it. You can also see that the collection and analysis of data can show that what people say may not be accurate, and that in itself might suggest further questions to ask. In the example, you might want to ask why women's work seems less hard or why people seem to ignore it. This question, based on the analysis of your previous work, would lead you to more research.

CONCLUSION

Thinking scientifically will put you in the proper attitude for thinking anthropologically, which in turn will allow you to think about human biology, archaeology, linguistics, or cultural anthropology. When you read about current evidence supporting a particular hypothesis, remember that it is not necessarily the last word. New evidence may be discovered that might force scientists to change their conclusions and perhaps ask new questions. That means that you should be skeptical and keep an open mind, realizing that there are different degrees of confidence given to each finding, and that science is self-correcting. Today's factoids may be tomorrow's corrected knowledge. And science continues, getting better and better at explaining that knowable world out there.

NOTE

1. Anthropologists do not all take the same approach to try to understand the world: humanistic anthropologists focus on cultural meaning, critical anthropologists focus on social evaluation and policy, and scientific anthropologists use the scientific method to explain what it is to be human. This chapter focuses on the scientific approach.

REFERENCES

BAHN, P.
2002. "A Most Mysterious Death." *Archaeology,* March/April: 54.
FOWLER, B.
2000. *Ice Man.* New York: Random House.
FREEMAN, D.
1983. *Margaret Mead and Samoa: The Making and Unmaking of an Anthropological Myth.* Cambridge, MA: Harvard University Press.
HARRIS, M.
1966. "The Cultural Ecology of India's Sacred Cattle." *Current Anthropology* 7: 51–66.
JOHNSON, A. W.
1975. "Time Allocation in a Machiguenga Community." *Ethnology* 14: 301–310.
MEAD, M.
1928. *Coming of Age in Samoa: A Psychological Study of Primitive Youth for Western Civilization.* New York: Morrow.
O'BRIAN, R.
1994. *The Peso and the Loom: The Political Economy of Maya Women's Work in Highland Chiapas, Mexico.* Ph.D. dissertation, UCLA.
RICE, P. C.
1981. "Prehistoric Venuses: Symbols of Motherhood or Womanhood?" *Journal of Anthropological Research* 37(4): 402–414.
1992. "The Boars from Altamira: Solving an Identity Problem." *Papers from the Institute of Archaeology, University College London* 3: 23–29.
RICE, P. C. and A. L. PATERSON
1988. "Anthropomorphs in Cave Art: An Empirical Assessment." *American Anthropologist* 90(3): 664–674.

STUDY QUESTIONS

1. Given what you know about the Ice Man (Ötzi), be deductive and generate a hypothesis about some aspect of his culture. How would you do your research under the scientific method? Would you be able to prove your findings?
2. Write three sentences, one each, of a hypothesis, a theory, and a law based on your experience. What confidence do you have for each relative to your statement?

CHAPTER 6

Thinking About Change

BIOLOGICAL EVOLUTION, CULTURE CHANGE,
AND THE IMPORTANCE OF SCALE

Jeffrey H. Cohen
Ohio State University

Jeffrey A. Kurland
Pennsylvania State University

Do your parents hate your favorite music? Do they ask you to turn it down or turn it off? Do they tell you that everything you listen to sounds the same? As you lower the volume, do you think to yourself, "Can't they hear the difference?" Now, imagine that a pair of anthropologists from a faraway planet show up at your door and enter your home. They ask to listen to your music. You play a new recording by your favorite band. After a song or two, they sit down with your parents and enjoy a few bars of your mother's Beethoven and your father's Beatles.

> The anthropologists listen a little longer and comment, "What is it with humans? All of your music sounds the same!"
>
> You respond, "Can't you hear the difference?"
>
> Your parents exclaim, "Don't tell us you like that noise."

The alien anthropologists sense an opportunity for an intergalactic exchange of ideas. They give you a mission: explain to them why not all human music is the same and why the differences that you hear matter. They remind you that they are not interested in your tastes or the disagreements you have with your parents. They want to understand the place and meaning of music in human culture and society.

In response to the aliens, your mother wonders, "Is the gamelan concert we heard last week at the university the same as Handel's *Messiah*?" Your parents lecture the aliens on the history of Western music from Gregorian chants of the eighth century to atonal music of the late twentieth century.

After 15 minutes you wake up and interrupt your parents, "What about the nineteenth-century gospel roots of rap and the folk music roots of grunge?"

THE STUDY OF CHANGE IN ANTHROPOLOGY: CHALLENGES AND POSSIBILITIES

If this vignette is interesting to you, welcome to the world of **culture change**. When anthropology was founded a little more than a century ago, one of its chief concerns was how to study change among human populations. Anthropology frames change in at least two ways: the **biological change** that our species has experienced over time and the sociocultural changes that separate and define human populations in the present. A third issue for anthropologists interested in the variability of the human species, human culture, and society was how best to define the *scale* of their analysis. In other words, before we could study change, we had to establish a measure against which change could be studied effectively. Anthropologists continue to debate how best to study change, and they continue to debate just what the proper scale of our investigations should be. This essay offers a glimpse of some key issues and concerns for the field from the perspectives of those of us who study biological evolution and those who study sociocultural change.

We can talk about change in many different ways. To illustrate just how hard it is to talk about change, let us return to the opening vignette concerning music. Are we interested in the changes that your mother and father went through as their musical tastes developed from the Beatles to Beethoven? Alternatively, are we interested in how the music of your generation grew from the songs of your parents? Do we want to know why we find gamelan in Indonesia and not in Western Europe? On the other hand, are we concerned with why all human populations make music? We might even ask whether humans are the only species on our planet that make music. What about the songs of birds and whales? Do these merit our interest?

Thus, there are various levels of complexity, different scales against which we want to talk about and investigate change. The first level focuses on individual changes, why you and your parents share different tastes. The second level focuses on historical patterns of change in the tastes of small groups. The third level posits questions that center on populations and asks where tastes sit in the social and cultural practices of a group. This would characterize the comment your mother made concerning the traditions of Western music and Indonesian gamelan, for example. Finally, the last level of analysis asks about human music in relation to other species and allows us to draw attention to the biological foundations of our behaviors.

EARLY APPROACHES TO CHANGE

Early researchers interested in the processes of change in human populations assumed that biological and sociocultural changes were analogous and that human populations were divisible by geography or arbitrary markers such as skin color or technological standards. The scale of much early work was therefore a population, not a culture, and certainly not the individual. **Social evolutionists**, including Herbert Spencer (1820–1903), argued that culture was a shared or universal attribute that evolved in a progressive, "ontogenetic" manner. Some cultures were infantile, whereas other cultures were quite mature (you can decide which level your music might fit). Because cultures evolved, they could be ranked according to their complexity, progress, and practices. Spencer used Victorian England as his ruler against which to measure most societies. He also argued that societies that did not "measure up" might catch up as they adopted the norms of English life. Models of "cultural evolution" were used to justify genocide against populations that were thought to be less evolved (biologically and culturally). Social evolutionists often borrowed Spencer's phrase "the survival of the fittest" and applied it to their analyses of culture. Cultures that could change and adapt would surely outlive and outperform those that were less evolved, or so thought social evolutionists.

Once again, let us return to our example of music. A social evolutionist would argue that the music you listen to is one indication of your culture's evolutionary status. Good music (in this case, classical music) is highly evolved. Your music (rock, rap, and grunge) is less evolved. Our interplanetary visitors would not hear major differences in musical styles; they are interested in universal patterns of behavior. In general, they would hear humans making music and ponder why so much of what they are hearing sounds the same.

If you think about this, you will realize that the question is not just about how culture and society change over time. The question is also about the scale of those changes. The social evolutionists were interested in variations between groups that they defined in largely arbitrary and geographically limited ways (North Americans, Africans, and Europeans, for example). They associated moral values with each group and used each group to illustrate the various stages in their hierarchy of "cultural evolution," with Europeans at the top, Africans and Native Australians at the bottom. By the way, social evolutionists felt that most North Americans fit somewhere below Europeans because they lacked the benefits of life in the British Commonwealth. In any case, the social evolutionists created a model that not only ranked human cultures but also created a morally weighted measure of those ranks.

Lewis Henry Morgan (1818–1881), a North American lawyer and ethnographer of the Iroquois Indians, constructed an important hierarchical model that divided human populations into three groups. What Morgan called "savage populations" had simple technology and were put at the bottom of the system. "Barbarians" fit in the middle of the system and were more evolved than savages but still lacked the moral and ethical standards of "civilized" populations. Civilized populations sat at the top of Morgan's ranking system. Civilized society (by which Morgan meant Victorian England) was characterized by "high" moral standards, codified legal systems, well-defined leadership, and such details as private property, wealth, fine art, and, of course, fine music. In this kind of a system, a high score on the ladder is morally better (and more highly evolved) than a low score. Nevertheless, for the alien anthropologists, we are all just humans: a pre-intergalactic species of sentient carbon-based life forms made up mostly of water. On the alien scale, we rank somewhere above pond scum, and we probably would not even come close to the rank of a civilized and cultured population.

HUMAN EVOLUTION AND BIOLOGICAL CHANGE

Today, we know that biological and sociocultural evolution are not the same and do not proceed in the same way. Culture does not follow biological logic, and biological evolution does not follow the progressive, directed path that can characterize sociocultural changes. How we know that has to do with the random nature of biological evolution is something we understand quite a bit better today than did the social evolutionists. Moreover, although biological evolution is a well-developed, technical subject, there are several basic concepts that you need to understand to appreciate the contrasts between biological and sociocultural change.

Victorian naturalist and scientist Charles Darwin (1809–1882) is most closely associated with our modern concept of biological evolution. However, it will not surprise you to learn that after a century and a half, we have a much better understanding of the process of evolution. Moreover, there no longer is any concern about finding evidence of the evolution of life on Earth. That is as undisputable as Newton's theory of gravitation or Boyle's theory of gases. Indeed, we now understand in detail how evolution occurs and what its consequences are.

Parents transmit genes to offspring. Genes are made up of a unique molecule, DNA, the physical basis of heredity. Because chemical and physical systems are never perfect, new combinations of DNA occur randomly and spontaneously, like the unique snowflakes that fall outside your dorm during winter. You can think of DNA as a set of rules that help an organism become a reproductively active adult. Sometimes, variants of DNA enhance an organism's fitness; however, most variants have no effect, and some are lethal. In the long run, the accumulation of genetic variants is evolution. Note that although genes are a key cause of the development of anatomy, physiology, and behavior, the environment constantly interacts with the DNA by means of biochemical processes to determine who and what you are. Darwin based his theory of evolution on a mechanism of *cumulative selection*. In other words, he believed that evolution was the retention of fitness-enhancing traits and the elimination of traits that do not favor fitness over long periods. The result is **adaptation**, **speciation**, and the ever-branching tree of life.

We know now that selection alone does not drive all evolutionary change. Selection occurs as does random processes, such as **mutation** and **drift**, that cause changes in genes or gene frequencies in each generation that can alter the characteristics of organisms over time. Finally, the movement of genes between populations, **gene flow**, can also change the genetic and trait structure of a local population.

The important point to remember is that biological evolution is the blind unfolding of particular physical and chemical systems in response to ever-changing environment in which they are situated. It is mechanism, not creation. There is no agency, no goal, and little direction to this natural process. Although human hair color and height seem to be *adaptive responses* to the environment because of selection, we know that these traits vary from place to place and from time to time. Over generations, increased height and elongated limbs are better responses to the hot, arid, open habitats of sub-Saharan Africa than short stature and short limbs. However, when our human ancestors migrated out of Africa, they evolved different body forms in new habitats, such as the short and more compact body of Arctic peoples. On the other hand, diet, activity, stress, and a host of other environmental factors affect adult height. Over many generations (1,000 to 10,000), height, hair color, and other traits may change back and forth without any obvious trend. Adaptation is a response to the local environment. Over the long haul, evolution isn't going anywhere! Thus, evolution for biologists is any change in the genetic properties of a population over time, whether that change leads to a "better" organism or not.

Given these concepts from evolutionary biology, is "cultural evolution" at all like biological evolution? The short answer is "No." Go back to the questions concerning music, and in place of style, think about the technology. How did your grandparents listen to a Beethoven symphony? They probably owned a series of thick, heavy, easily breakable, monophonic 78-rpm records. By the time your parents bought a Beethoven symphony, it was probably pressed on a single, stereophonic, 33-1/3-rpm, vinyl record. If you want to listen to a Beethoven symphony today, you might purchase a CD that includes three different versions of the same piece. Alternatively, you can download an MP3, without using any kind of disk.

CULTURE CHANGE

Unlike biological evolution, social and cultural changes are driven by agents, human beings, who set goals and then act to reach them. In general, social and cultural changes are the result of conscious processes, and although we are not necessarily good at predicting the outcomes of change, because we learn norms from our parents, siblings, friends, and surroundings, we can learn how to make changes. The point is, unlike biological change that is largely random, we can talk about the progress that comes from sociocultural change. Comparing ten 78-rpm records with 5 megabytes on an MP3 player, you can clearly distinguish which is better. It is important to remember that although we can plan for change in society, such changes are built on shared concepts of value and worth. You can ask yourself why we would pursue social and cultural changes if we did not value them. Nevertheless, this also means that points of disagreement will arise as changes occur. Don't forget, your parents probably think your favorite music is profoundly bad; in other words, it is not part of a progressive pattern of change. If that gives you pause, just wait. When you have children, you'll probably feel the same way about their favorite music.

Let us go a little farther with this point. Say you are a collector of 78-rpm records. Are you less evolved because you enjoy the sound and ambience of the recordings rather than the sterility of a modern MP3? This question returns us to the crux of the problem when it comes to the study of change. What is the scale of our investigations, and what are we hoping to learn?

American anthropologists reacted to social evolutionists in the early twentieth century and quickly pointed out how inappropriate ranked models of human social development were. One approach favored by North Americans was to follow how particular traits and practices diffused through a region; this approach usually is described as **historical particularism** and is associated with anthropologists such as Franz Boas (1858–1942), Alfred Kroeber (1876–1960), and to a lesser extent Margaret Mead (1901–1978). These anthropologists used collections of material culture from an area to document how traits and practices developed. They would ask, Where was a practice established? How was it adopted by other cultures and populations? How did a trait change in its adoption? What they did not care for were questions that focused on individual tastes. Thus, like their intergalactic counterparts, they were not interested in your musical tastes; instead, they were interested in where your musical taste came from. To use their terminology, they were interested in knowing how patterns of use and tradition **diffused** from one region to another. Historical particularists focused on how music moved from one place to another. They would investigate why gamelan is found in Indonesia and not in Western Europe.

To get a better feel for how diffusion works, let's return to the example with which we began. Music styles follow diffusional paths. One group borrows from another and in the process creates something unique. Here is one example. Cohen works in rural Mexico in the state of Oaxaca with a native population called the Zapotec, a term that defines them by the language they speak. The pre-Hispanic Zapotec, those who were around before the arrival of the Spanish, had music, but they lacked instruments beyond forms of drums and flutes—at least that is what we know from the archaeological record. Once the Spanish arrived, the Zapotec (like most native groups) quickly adopted the instruments and musical traditions, among other things, of their conquerors. They adapted the music of their conquerors to reflect their own interests. Today, you can purchase music sung in Zapotec and played by native musicians on modern Western instruments. Sometimes they incorporate jazz and classical motifs. You can also find Western musicians who have borrowed from the Zapotec and sing in their language.

Other approaches have developed that replaced historical particularism and diffusional models through the twentieth century. Some anthropologists coped with the difficulties involved in studying change by ignoring it. *Structural functionalists* such as A. R. Radcliffe-Brown (1881–1955) were interested in how social systems maintained their status quo over time. A society was characterized as something like a car or a boat, and the key was to understand why a society would run smoothly over time like a boat and would not sink. Other anthropologists developed hierarchical models of social evolution that focused on technological change on one hand (e.g., Leslie White, 1900–1975) or argued that while societies evolved, evolution took place at a local level and in a multitude of ways as local systems adapted to their particular ecologies (such as Julian Steward [1902–1972]). Although few scholars embraced the technological models of social evolution, the local evolutionary models are still with us under the heading of **cultural ecology**.

Anthropologists have gone off in a multitude of directions since the mid-twentieth century, founding symbolic, interpretive, postmodern, and economic approaches, among others. Nevertheless, how to deal with change continues to captivate the field. Many contemporary models of change approach the subject through an ethnographic lens. In other words, anthropologists use our key research tools, including **participant observation**, to understand the history, pattern, and process of change. By constructing ethnographic models of change, we are able to understand how a society or culture comes to appear as it does. We include historical data to understand why certain attributes may look the way they do. For example, a population's music may lack certain scales or particular instruments. We discover why the gaps are present through ethnographic research. Maybe it is a result of diffusion, or the lack of diffusion of a particular trait. Maybe a sociopolitical or socioeconomic event influenced the group, and one outcome was a change in musical traditions. Perhaps the issue is one of religion, and the society placed bans on certain types of musical expression, or perhaps only a certain type was encouraged. In any case, through careful ethnography, anthropologists are able to trace patterns of change.

SCALE AND CHANGE

The question of scale is crucial to the results of any study. Are we interested in a specific group? Do we want to know about one culture's practices? Alternatively, are we interested in intercultural variation? Maybe the question is one of gendered responses. For example, are there kinds of music made by men but not by women in your study population? Anthropologist Colin Turnbull spent many years with the BaMbuti of central Africa. He tells a story about how certain horns or flutes that are important in rituals to "calm the forest" for the BaMbuti became the property and responsibility of men. It seems that in the distant past, these horns or flutes originally belonged to women, but men stole them and hid them. As they claimed the horns and flutes from the women, men also claimed the mystical powers that were associated with the horns and flutes. The job for the anthropologist is to understand this example of change and why it is important. If you want to know more about this switch, you can read Turnbull's book *The Forest People.*

One point we have avoided is individual change and the question of why you like the particular music you like. Maybe you find yourself wondering, "How do I study individual change?" You might even think, "Well, I'm always changing, you know that line, I'm getting better every day in every way." You can complicate the question and add, "I'm the result of evolutionary process that is ongoing, so why aren't I evolving? Where does this leave me? How can I talk coherently about change? Where do I draw the line on what change is?"

DO INDIVIDUALS EVOLVE?

This brings up another point that we want you to understand: when anthropologists talk about change, they are talking about changes that occur in populations, or groups of people. In fact, one of the points on which biological and sociocultural models tend to agree is that both areas are interested in changes that occur for a population, not for individuals. Think of it this way: populations evolve, and groups go through continuous sociocultural change. Individuals can change, too, but individuals do not evolve biologically. If you spent your life in a swimming pool, you would not grow webbed feet; nor would your children. You'd be wet, but you wouldn't change at a fundamental biological level. Nevertheless, if you wanted to live in water, you could adapt your sociocultural practices to facilitate the changes you wanted to make. For the anthropologist, you might be interesting but not a good subject for study, unless of course you convince lots of people to join you and live under water. What the individual does is interesting, but from an anthropological perspective, we don't tend to focus on individual tastes except in how they illustrate group norms. We use ethnographic fieldwork and genetics to focus on populations, and we work with individuals to understand the range of the patterns that we hope to define. We are able to control and cut through the background noise and variation that characterize individual patterns by studying and talking about change in terms of populations.

CULTURAL RELATIVISM AND CHANGE

The ranking and subjectivity that characterized the social evolutionists still haunt much work on culture change. It is extremely hard not to judge and measure a population's sociocultural systems against our own. For example, suppose the alien anthropologists choose you to visit their world and to listen to their music in an effort to conduct a comparative study of the two populations. You step off the ramp leading from the wormhole transportation system and realize that you are hungry. You want a pizza. "Pizza?" your hosts ask, "What is pizza? How about these lovely tubeworms we eat lightly tossed in a rich sesame sauce?" The aliens like to eat the worms raw, but they are trying to be nice. This might seem a trivial illustration, but the point is important. It is extremely hard to study a foreign society or cultural system without judging that system.

Some anthropologists argue that in such a situation, you must exercise complete **cultural relativism**, and they are mostly correct. Cultural relativism asks anthropologists and investigators to try to put aside their own cultural beliefs and social rules and to try to understand what is happening around them from a native's perspective. Cultural relativism is hard to manage. What if you need to spend a year with the aliens? For an entire year, everything you've grown up with is missing: your favorite foods, your favorite movies, your favorite music. Moreover, all that time, you have to try your best to understand what is going on from the native's point of view. This is what anthropologists do to understand society and culture. Getting beyond our sociocultural biases is one of the reasons we do field-work. The goal is to understand society and culture from the native's perspective. Given this, we want to make one point clear: being culturally relative does not mean we are morally relative. In other words, a cultural relativist doesn't say, "Anything goes!" We will leave moral relativism for the philosophers to debate. However, as you learn about cultures and societies from around the world (and maybe someday from other worlds), we want you to remain as open-minded as you can and to work hard to limit the amount of ranking and valuation.

A LAST EXAMPLE AND THOUGHT

Let's proceed to an example of cultural change. We started this chapter by asking what kind of music you like, and now we will return to music. Do you like the same kind of music that you liked when you were in grade school or high school? Would you describe your taste in music as changing over time? Has your taste improved? In addition, why has your taste changed? Have you heard new genres of music or new artists? The kinds of changes that characterize how your taste in music develops probably seem quite progressive. Maybe you would describe the music you listen to today as more complex than the music you listened to as a child.

In fact, changing tastes in music can be directional. In other words, you can learn to like a new kind of music. You can even take a very active role in exposing yourself to new music. However, the change can also be random and arbitrary. You are walking across campus and you hear something different coming from a dorm window. You find out what it is, and there you are—a random act of change! Change in this case can be random or directional, but your parents might not think it is progressive.

Add a layer of complication to the question of cultural change. We know that you like a certain kind of music. You know how your tastes have changed. However, if we are interested in cultural patterns, how can we cut through the fact that no two people share the exact same tastes in music? Use yourself as an example: do you share the exact same tastes in music as your friends? If we want to get deeply philosophical, we can ask, "How do you know you even hear the music the same?"

Anthropologists resolve the problem of individual variation in a couple of different ways. First, we never talk to only one person. Instead, we take a sample of a group of people and call those people our **informants**. There might be one extremely useful informant, a key informant, but if we are worth our weight in ethnography, we will talk to a representative, random sample of a group. By talking to a random group that is representative of a population, we are more likely to hear about a good deal of the variation that is present in a population. We can also use the responses of a random group of informants to understand where people agree and disagree about cultural practices.

We hope that this brief review of how anthropologists study change and why biological and sociocultural changes are different has been useful. We want to encourage you to practice what you have learned: look around you and think about how patterns change over time. From food to clothing to music, there is an amazing amount to study: you can design your own diffusional models of music or clothing, or maybe the spread of pizza and bagels from East Coast cities such as New York to the entire country. You don't need to go to some foreign setting for this to be interesting; just think of how slang moves across our country. That is a diffusional study of culture change you can do from your desk. But don't stop with the easy stuff; think about the tough issues, too. Why do humans tend to want to associate biological and sociocultural evolution when they have such different processes? Why are social evolutionary models so persuasive, and why have these models been used to promote hatred? These are tough questions, but they are questions that we must answer.

STUDY QUESTIONS

1. You are a graduate student specializing in cultural anthropology and find yourself in the New Guinea highlands about to study culture change there during the last 20 years when your group changed from a "stone age" culture to a global economy. Which approach would you use for this study and why, and what might be some of your findings?

2. Reflect on changes in some of your personal likes and dislikes in your relatively short life so far. What kinds of books did you like as a child versus what you like to read now? What about movies, TV programs, and yes, music. What does this suggest for the scale of change in modern times?

CHAPTER 7

Why Do Anthropological Experts Disagree?

Anne Campbell

Fairfield University

Patricia C. Rice

West Virginia University

What image comes to mind when you hear the name Ozzy Osbourne? Do you see a burnt out rocker advertising cell phones or a hard rock icon who shocked the world when he bit the head off a bat during a concert?[1] Are *Grand Theft Auto I, II, III,* and *IV* great video games or a threat to society because they glorify violence, teach children to steal cars, and encourage criminal behavior (Crowley 2008)? Is the TV series *24* one of the best dramas on television, or is it a front for a conservative political agenda (Mayer 2007)? Does it normalize torture and support the misuse of government power, or is it merely a work of fiction designed to entertain? Did woolly mammoths talk, and if they did, did they sound like Ray Romano? The answers to these questions depend on the age, sex, and previous experience of individual consumers of "popular culture." Whereas 3- to 5-year-olds would agree after seeing *Ice Age 2* that woolly mammoths did talk, even speaking English, and made dandy pets, adults would not. Whereas members of the gaming community might think that *Grand Theft Auto IV* is a masterpiece worthy of an Oscar, most adults do not. And whereas most adults consider *24* a fast-acted drama, critics do not. And there is probably no consensus on the phenomenon called Ozzy Osbourne relative to categories related to sex, age, or previous experience.

Cultural anthropologists who specialize in analyzing cultural phenomena in their own and in other cultures are also involved in analyzing the cultural context of Ozzy, Buffy, or woolly mammoths. But instead of only having biases based on their age, sex, or previous experiences, cultural anthropologists also have biases based on how they interpret cultural phenomena, and they would probably not agree with each other on any of the questions posed earlier. Why not?

What image comes to mind when you hear the word "Neandertal"? Do you imagine a slouching, hairy beast, wearing a bedraggled animal skin with one shoulder bare, with a club in one hand, dragging a woman by her hair into a cave, saying "ugh" all the while? Although we cannot view Neandertals directly, we have fossils that might indicate a slouched posture or speech, and we have artifacts that might indicate that they had clubs or tools that could be used to scrape animal hides for clothing. Biological anthropologists and archaeologists have to interpret those fossil and artifactual materials, and they do not necessarily agree on those interpretations. Why not?

As a start, Thomas Kuhn, the leading philosopher of science in the mid-1900s, wrote that what people see depends on what they look at and what their "previous visual and conceptual experience has taught" them to see (1962:111). That statement is as true today as when Kuhn wrote it 48 years ago. What we look at is not the same as what we see. This observation explains in part why anthropological experts disagree.

To understand the difference between looking and seeing, mentally put an apple on the table in front of you and mentally invite two friends to observe that apple with you. ("Observation" is used here as a neutral term.) Don't talk about the apple; you may walk around it but cannot pick it up or manipulate it. Take 5 minutes to write down your observations and then compare notes with your two friends.

Did you all write down a color? Was it the same color and in the same detail? Did you compare the color with a formal color chart? Did you recognize what kind of apple it is? Did you all observe size, and if so, did you say the same thing about its size? Probably not. Some of you observed color, but maybe not all; some may have matched its color with a color chart, but others probably just noted a generic term, "red" or "green." Some probably noted that it was a McIntosh or a Delicious, but others didn't. In short, no two people will see the same things or ask the same questions, much less use the same methods to attempt to find answers. Looking at the apple is one thing; seeing it involves using what Kuhn calls "visual-conceptual experience."

Now ask yourself, "Because we were all looking at the same thing, why didn't we all see the same thing?" If you had been allowed to discuss the investigation beforehand, you all might have agreed on what to observe, what questions to ask, and even what methods would be best to use to ask them, but you were not allowed to do that. Some obvious answers to the "Why did you differ question" might be that one friend is a horticulture major and knows apple variety names by merely looking at them and the rest of you don't, one of you is a fashion design major and is particularly experienced in differentiating colors, and one of you is a math major and used to assessing size. Female observers might be more interested in color, male observers might be more interested in size, older observers might be more interested in the variety, and younger observers might be interested only in eating the apple. Obviously, previous experience is an important variable in terms of what each of you observed and saw, but so are age and sex. These are all variables that resulted in bias, assumptions, and preconceptions that changed what you looked at to what you saw. They were the lens between the reality of the apple and what you each saw. And these same variables are part of the reason why anthropologists disagree with each other on scientific issues.

The cultural background of individuals can affect what they see as well and this applies to scientists as well as "apple observers." Let's remove many of the biases of two scientists and make them the same age and sex, and give them the same amount of scientific training and experience. One of the scientists is a Western scientist from either a European or American culture and the other is a Japanese scientist. They are both going to study black-and-white colobus monkeys in Kenya. Follow them as each views the same group of monkeys, and you will see two different versions of monkey observation because each scientist was raised in a different culture. The Japanese observer will see the total monkey group first, noting demographic numbers of how many total monkeys there are, how many males versus females, how many of each age group; then the Japanese scientist will observe interactions of groups, then dyads (two monkeys), and finally will observe individual monkeys. The Western scientist will observe a single monkey first, then other individuals, then dyads, groups, and the interactions of the entire group. Note a correlation in this pattern with how scientists (and all other people) will address an envelope: in Japan, the scientist starts with Japan, then the city, street and number, and finally the scientist's name. Of course the Western scientist puts his or her name first, then the number and street, city, state, country, and zip code.[2] Whether a scientist focuses on the big picture or the small picture may be initially caused by the culture he or she grew up in, in this case a kind of "upside down paradigm."

BIAS, SCIENCE, AND ANTHROPOLOGY

It does not matter whether a scientist is a physicist, biologist, geologist, or anthropologist, and it does not matter whether the anthropologist is a cultural anthropologist, a biological anthropologist, or an archaeologist; these same variables will cause at least some bias in the investigation of any scientific arena. Male scientists and female scientists are not necessarily interested in answering the same questions about the same phenomenon because they don't necessarily see them as having equal importance; their sex alone may affect the questions they ask and the methods of inquiry they use. In the case of cultural anthropologists, sex may also influence the kind of data to which they have access. Older and younger scientists are not necessarily interested in answering the same questions in the same ways, either. And one's past experience is always an important variable in regard to the questions asked and methods used. These differences explain in part why experts disagree.

Another variable that leads to bias is inherent in the nature of science. Early scientists assumed that they were capable of clearing their minds of all preconceptions and bias and achieving total objectivity. As a result, they believed great "truths" of science would emerge at the end of their investigations. These early scientists believed there was a real world out there that could be observed and seen directly, and they went about doing science with that belief in mind (Chamberlain and Hartwig 1999; Clark 1993). These early scientists are called *strict empiricists*. Although some scientists still believe they are unbiased, strict empiricism was and is a myth. Sex, age, culture, and individual experience will always influence what humans see and do.

By the early twentieth century, most scientists operated under the belief that there still was a real world out there but that it could not be observed or seen directly; additionally, they believed that what they observed had to be interpreted and therefore would always be somewhat biased, but they believed that precise data collecting, hypothesis generating, and appropriate testing would yield results that would be as close as they could come to "reality" and "true knowledge" about the world. Philosophers of science call these scientists **logical positivists** (Binford and Sabloff 1982). Thomas Kuhn believes this is how most scientists actually do science today, suggesting that scientists "get in the middle" of their science, whether they want to or not and whether they realize it or not (Chamberlain and Hartwig 1999). Most scientists probably would grudgingly agree with this perspective, and it is the one taken here: scientists attempt to be as unbiased as they can, but preconceptions, assumptions, subjectivity, and bias are always present in one form or another and to one extent or another. (Some modern scientists do not believe there is a real world out there at all to discover. Some believe there are numerous worlds out there, not just one. And some believe that one or more worlds can't be discovered well enough to even try. These critical theory advocates are in the minority and are regarded by many as being highly critical of other scientists but as not having advanced science using their philosophy. They will not be discussed further.)

INTELLECTUAL TRADITIONS, CULTURE, AND PARADIGMS

To get back to the question of why experts disagree on anthropological issues, differences in sex, age, and individual experience are at least partially the cause of the subjective lens through which they view their world. There is an additional anthropological bias, called the **intellectual tradition**, that is also behind how we interpret what we observe. The intellectual tradition bias is stronger in paleoanthropology (archaeology, prehistory, and human evolution) than in cultural anthropology, although cultural anthropology has not escaped different ways to conceptualize culture.

The two intellectual traditions that have arisen in Western science that affect anthropology and how anthropologists think have historical roots going back to the last quarter of the nineteenth century (Clark and Willermet 1995). What is called the Old World (OW) tradition exists in England and on the European continent and has its intellectual roots mainly in history, nationalism, and natural sciences, and also, depending on the anthropological specialty, in geology, paleontology, and sociology. What is called the New World (NW) tradition exists in North America and has its roots in Native American cultural studies that existed at the time anthropology became a discipline in the United States a little more than a hundred years ago. Under the OW tradition, most British and European anthropologists see human evolution and human prehistory as history projected into the preliterate past, with the processes that caused human evolution and culture change being the same in the past as today. Under this tradition, most cultural anthropologists see modern "other cultures" as different from their own and focus on finding and explaining those differences. By contrast, under the NW tradition, most American anthropologists see human evolution and prehistory as entities in their own right; most cultural anthropologists see modern "other cultures" as they exist in our backyards as Native Americans and focus on finding and explaining the similarities that exist in all cultures (Binford and Sabloff 1982; Clark 1993).

Experts learn their particular tradition as they learn their science; obviously, which tradition an expert learns and supports depends on the side of the Atlantic Ocean on which he or she is trained. In anthropology, students take a first anthropology course, choose to pursue it as a career, and begin to unconsciously pick up some of the intellectual tradition of the instructor. And the students continue to be immersed in this single tradition (usually without knowing it), so that by the time they have earned their Ph.D. degrees and are ready to begin their careers, they are steeped in that tradition.

One of the major reasons why OW and NW intellectual traditions differ is because each views the concept of culture somewhat differently. Beginning in the 1800s, with the development of the social sciences, OW anthropologists regarded "a culture" and "cultures" as being the same as "a people" and "peoples," each having its own unique and internally consistent package of material objects such as clothing and food, language, and physical type. Indeed, under the OW tradition, experts think of "the English People" as a homogeneous group of people wearing similar clothing and eating "bangers, mash, and boiled cabbage," all speaking the Queen's English, and all being tall and light skinned, with light brown hair. The fact that this stereotype is not very accurate is beside the point. The point is that under this tradition, "a people" connotes a multifaceted unit of language, culture, and biology, all tied together as a neat package. Along with this view go ideas that logically stem from this OW view of culture: associated traits (material objects and functionally related biological traits) constantly occur together, but blending or mixing of traits does not occur. When change occurs, it does so rapidly as if one "people" somehow replaced another (**punctuated equilibrium**), and the result over time and space is *discontinuity* in both biology and culture (Clark 1993; 2002).

By contrast, NW anthropologists view "a culture" and "cultures" as being made up of different levels of social, ethnic, and linguistic groups. They also see groups of people as being made up of different traits (material objects and biological traits) that are not and were not necessarily always associated with each other. Traits and complexes can occur in many areas, and the blend or mix of traits is common and to be expected. Change usually occurs gradually as inventions and shared ideas on the cultural side and mutations and natural selection on the biological side add up, but when there is rapid change, it is caused by a change in environment (**Darwinian gradualism**); finally, the result over time and space is *continuity* in both biology and culture (Clark 1993; 2002).

If preconceptions, subjectivity, and bias (due to sex, age, culture, and previous experiences) are added to intellectual tradition, the result is what is called a **paradigm** (Clark 1993). A paradigm includes the sum of the different biases scientists have between reality and what the scientist sees as well as the intellectual tradition the scientist has grown up with and defends. A paradigm is a kind of frame through which the scientist views his or her world and as such is logically consistent. Paradigms usually are called by the name of their intellectual tradition, but remember that paradigms include the collective bias taken to the scientific table. Paradigm differences are the consummate reason why experts disagree even when there are the same things to see.

PARADIGMS IN CULTURAL ANTHROPOLOGY

Paradigms influence how one conceptualizes what one is going to study. They also influence the methods by which data are documented. For example, cultural anthropologists gather data by observation. However, what they see and how they interpret it depends in part on the paradigm through which they view the world.

Cultural anthropologists from different intellectual traditions could study the same cultural event and focus on different components of that event. Depending on which elements they emphasized, the anthropologists could gather data that would result in different interpretations of group behavior or different understandings of the cultural significance of that event. For example, if an anthropologist were interested in power relationships and change and focused data collection on cultural institutions and their interrelationships, he or she might not pay attention to child-rearing practices that could have provided insight into the cultural transmission of belief systems that reinforce and reproduce the existing power structures. Conversely, if the anthropologist focused on child-rearing practices, he or she might not realize their implications for the maintenance of the status quo within the larger society. Does this make either data set inaccurate or incomplete, or are they different descriptions of different qualities of the same "apple" called culture? As experts attempt to answer this question, they will probably disagree.

In addition to these issues, experts may disagree on the interpretation of particular data. One reason is that the interpretation is often made in light of **theories** that are constructed to attempt to explain the larger paradigm in which the anthropologists were trained and through which they view the world. (See Chapter 4 for more discussion of theories.) In the late 1800s, for example, cultural anthropologists shared the belief "that evolution meant human progress from primitive (savage) through an intermediate (barbarian) to a civilized stage" (Goodenough 2002:427). This "progress" was thought to be universal, and interpretations of cultural data were used to develop theories of cultural differences that fit that belief. J. Boggs (2002) argues that remnants of this paradigm can still be seen in contemporary debates regarding U.S. policy toward Native Americans. Throughout the twentieth century, the theories that guided cultural anthropologists changed as different generations gained knowledge and insights regarding human behavior. With these changes have come debates between experts who adhere to different theories. Debates include discussions of the adequacy of data gathered, the accuracy of the theory as a tool to interpret the cultural change, and the value of findings and interpretations as contributions to our overall understanding of the human condition.

Adequacy of the data depends in part on the representativeness of the events that cultural anthropologists observe and in which they participate. One cannot document well what one cannot see or experience, and one cannot document at all the elements of culture that one does not even know exist. It is here that age and gender play a key role in understanding why experts disagree.

Because of their sex and age, anthropologists may not be aware of or have access to critical cultural information and events. Both of these factors are illustrated in Diane Freedman's work in Romania (1986). She began her study of dance and gender roles as a married woman and was able to document the roles and norms pertinent to that status. Through her husband's activities and his interaction with the men, she gained access to the men's perspective as well. When she returned to her fieldwork after the death of her husband, her status changed to that of widow. This change gave her access to another dimension of female gender roles, that of caretaker for the ill and dying. Older widows in the community with whom she had little contact when she was married wanted to learn of her experiences and in turn shared theirs, as well as their perspectives on death. When Freedman's period of mourning ended during her fieldwork, her status changed overnight to one of single, eligible woman. This change made it possible for her to interact with young unmarried women and to participate in activities appropriate for that group. She was able to learn "about customs and spells for attracting men as husbands and dance partners" (1986:351), knowledge and activities to which she had had limited or no access in her prior statuses as wife and widow.

Sex also affects the importance given to cultural events and the ways in which those events are interpreted. This influence can be seen in differences between male and female perspectives within a community. It can also be seen in a comparison of ethnographies written by male and female anthropologists who have studied the same cultural group. In *Headhunter's Heritage*, for example, Robert Murphy (1960) documents in detail the Mundurucu culture (Amazonia) through the lens of male activities and ideology. Only 10 of the 193 pages are devoted to a discussion of women and family. The concept of gossip receives a paragraph and is characterized as "the chief form of expression of antagonism among the women" (116–117). In *Women of the Forest*, Yolanda and Robert Murphy (1985) examine the differences between the women's and men's perspectives, and more than 160 pages detail aspects of the women's world not found in Robert's previous work. Yolanda learned through her interactions with the women that gossip plays several essential roles in the social life of the community. First, it provides "valuable information about people, . . . events in other communities, and nearly every other subject conceivable in their restricted worlds" (159–160). It also is an informal indicator of importance within the group: "it may be worrisome for a Mundurucu woman to know she is being talked about, but it would be a disaster if she were to discover that nobody was talking about her" (160). Yolanda documented the hostile uses of gossip, but she found that negative gossip that focused on sexual exploits was done for a reason. Sexual promiscuity threatened the "moral solidarity of the females." Rather than being just an indicator of antagonism between women, it was in fact a powerful "negative sanction exercised by women over their wayward member to bring her back into line before the men staged a gang rape" (160–161). Gossip thus provided women with an important means for timely intervention designed to prevent extreme punishment for the violation of cultural norms. The influence of sex on differences in data gathered and interpreted, as illustrated by the Murphys' work, provides insights into some of the reasons why experts disagree.

PARADIGMS IN PALEOANTHROPOLOGY

Paleoanthropology is defined as the science of humans in the past: biological anthropology concentrates on human evolution, and archaeology concentrates on human prehistory. Because scientists do not have a time machine to use to go back to prehistoric times and places to view paleocultures in action (as cultural anthropologists can do today) or see what populations were interbreeding with other populations (as modern biologists can), common sense suggests that there is a large and fertile ground for disagreement among paleoanthropologists. Under the OW paradigm, most European and British paleoanthropologists view the human past as being made up of people living in distinct groups that were homogeneous in material traits, language, and biology and that did not mix with other groups, and when biological or cultural change occurred, it was quick in time and space because of invasions or replacements. The emphasis is on discontinuity. Most OW paleoanthropologists emphasize differences in material objects and morphology and give a separate name to each population in time or space. This is called **splitting**. By contrast, under the NW paradigm, most American paleoanthropologists view the human past as being made up of people living in groups that met up with other groups deliberately for mating purposes or accidentally when their hunting territories overlapped; they exchanged ideas, material items, and genes in the process, and when change occurred, it was slow and continuous through time and change was small between groups living at the same time. The emphasis is on continuity. NW paleoanthropologists emphasize similarities in material objects and morphology and **lump** populations together under single names (Clark 1993).

Let us now focus on one ongoing controversy in paleoanthropology and put intellectual traditions together with biases (that is, paradigms) to try to discover why experts on the two sides of the Atlantic disagree over this single issue. The controversy is over the position of Neandertals in the evolution of modern humans. Basically, the question is, "Did Neandertals contribute anything to our ancestry?" The OW paradigm claims they did not contribute to our ancestry. OW proponents agree that there was an up to 10,000-year overlap of the two populations living in the Near East and in Europe—the last 10,000 years of Neandertals and the first 10,000 years of modern humans—but they firmly believe that the two populations did not interbreed[3] or exchange material objects. These experts conclude that the two groups did not influence each other culturally, linguistically, or biologically, that there was no intermingling or hybridization, and that change (that is, the demise of Neandertals at about 30,000 years ago) came quickly. These experts assign the term *Homo neandertalensis* rather than *Homo sapiens* (for modern humans) to demonstrate their belief in discontinuity, splitting, and separate species status. All of these points are consistent and make logical sense once the paradigm is understood.

By contrast, the NW paradigm claims Neandertals did have a role to play in the evolution of modern humans, with proponents suggesting that the two populations were interbreeding, although how much is difficult to ascertain. These experts conclude that the two populations did influence each other by exchanging some material objects and ideas as well as genes, and that change—the demise of Neandertals—was primarily through interbreeding, with both archaeological and biological Neandertal traits slowly disappearing by 30,000 years ago. These experts assign the term *Homo sapiens neandertalensis* to the Neandertal population, confirming their belief in continuity and only subspecies status. Again, these points are consistent and make logical sense once the paradigm is understood.

Now you know why experts differ on the Neandertal question, and the stage is set for proponents in each paradigm to do science. But experts from each paradigm ask different questions, look at different data, use different methods, take different measurements, and come to different conclusions. Additionally, experts accuse the other "side" of using bad, fragmentary, or incorrect data, using bad methods, being contradictory and misinformed, coming up with wrong conclusions, and not understanding the other side. Proponents of each paradigm also say they have tested their paradigm and found it to be superior to the other at answering the question and claim that the other side just can't see it (Smith and Harrold 1997). As one example, let's look at data and measurements. In 1997, Cathy Willermet looked at the 39 publications written during the previous 15 years by experts supporting one or the other paradigm and found that when 680 data points representing 61 variables were taken on 55 Neandertal fossils, only 11 percent of the measurements were used by both sides, leaving 89 percent of the data essentially not usable (Clark and Willermet 1997). The choice of fossils used in analysis and the weight given to each trait also vary between the supporters of the two paradigms. Additionally, in paleoanthropology, the dates of fossil and artifact data are vital to answering any question, and unfortunately the best dating technique (carbon-14 in this case) is at the extreme end (40,000 years ago) of its accuracy; so when conflicting dates are given, the one chosen often depends on how well it fits a particular paradigm.

Under these circumstances, it is no wonder that a British expert, steeped in "culture as a people," probably will see discontinuity between Neandertals and modern humans and see separate species status. By contrast, it is no wonder that an American expert probably will see continuity between Neandertals and modern humans and see only subspecies status. And this is generally the way it is. Even though these experts have access to the same fossil and artifactual data, some look at the data through the lens of the OW paradigm and some through the NW paradigm. With few exceptions, British and European paleoanthropologists claim Neandertals were not part of our ancestry, and with the same few exceptions, American paleoanthropologists claim that Neandertals were involved in our ancestry. When new data and even new kinds of data are introduced, proponents of each side interpret them as supporting only their paradigm.

Under these circumstances, it is also understandable why François Bordes, France's leading archaeologist in the mid-1900s, decided that the entire collection of Neandertal flint tools in Europe and the Middle East, which he called Mousterian industries, could be classified into four types (called facies, each with a name) based on the absence or presence and the frequency of numerous kinds of tools (Bordes 1968). Although these four types were not located in four distinct areas or in four chronological time periods, he still maintained that they represented four tribal groups that did not interact with each other. One could envision four independent peoples wandering Europe and the Middle East for thousands of years without exchanging tool recipes or genes or even being able to say "Hi" in passing. Bordes viewed prehistoric Europe through the OW paradigm. Given his reputation, his scheme was accepted until Lewis Binford, an American archaeologist, questioned the four-tribe notion. The argument over whether the four categories represent four cultural groups or four tool functions came to a standstill in the mid-1960s. Which answer you choose to believe depends on your paradigm (Clark 2002).

A final "why" question is in order here: "Why does each side continue to adhere so strongly to its paradigm?" Consider the following possibility. In the last 200 years, Europe has seen many conflicts on its land, from world wars to continent-wide wars to internal wars, and has seen entire populations—"peoples" in the OW culture, language, and biology package—being physically moved many miles away or being exterminated, with other populations coming in and displacing original populations, over and over again. This history reinforces discontinuity as the norm in the OW. By contrast, America has not seen such turmoil. The two world wars were not fought on American soil, the Civil War did not displace entire populations, and although there has been much immigration of people from the rest of the world, whole populations were not moved or replaced because of it. It is easier to think of continuity, the exchange of ideas and genes, and a resultant "melting pot" as the norm in the NW (Clark 1993).

CONCLUSION

So where do we and should we stand as anthropologists relative to science in general, paradigms, the Neandertal question, and cultural disagreements? Kuhn is correct that scientists operate with bias and subjectivity, knowingly or unknowingly, because each is a member of only one sex, is at a certain age in life, has had unique experiences, and has been brought up in only one cultural and intellectual tradition; therefore, each scientist views science through a single paradigm, one that does not necessarily agree with other scientists' paradigms, and that causes disagreement. As for existing paradigms in any discipline such as anthropology, Kuhn predicts that they will not change quickly. In regard to the Neandertal question, several scientists not directly involved in the controversy have suggested that the two paradigms will continue until the major proponents of each side have died. But even then, their many students will carry on the fight just because of entrenched positions. Each side has proponents who seem to think that if they yell louder and more often than the other side, they will win the argument. Although new fossil and artifact data and correct dates for all of the materials are welcome, they will be evaluated by each side in terms of its preferred paradigm and will not solve the paradigm dilemma.

That experts disagree seems to be a theme that permeates anthropology in general. Cultural anthropologists are no more in agreement about cultural phenomena and how to interpret them than paleoanthropologists are in interpreting past human events. It may not be something we are proud of, but it is a commonality. And disagreement is common to any endeavor that attempts to be scientific; it comes with the territory. As a former president of the American Anthropological Association, James Peacock, wrote in 1986, "many anthropologists would deny that there is any overriding perspective [guiding all anthropological inquiry;] . . . many anthropologists seek some unifying perspective" (93). The one thing all anthropologists have in common is a search for knowledge about the human condition, past and present, biologically and culturally. A second commonality is that in our search for knowledge, we can—and must—disagree.

NOTES

1. The authors have been told several different stories about whether the bat was real or plastic, live or dead.
2. This information is from "Negotiating Science: Internationalization and Japanese Primatology" by P. Asquith, and "Traditions of the Kyoto School of Field Primatology in Japan" by H. Takasaki. In *Primary Encounters* (2000) edited by S. C. Strum and L. M. Fedigan. Chicago, IL: University of Chicago Press.
3. Some OW experts admit there might have been a bit of interbreeding but believe it was unimportant and had no effect on either population.

REFERENCES

BINFORD, L. R. and J. A. SABLOFF

1982. "Paradigms, Systematics and Archaeology." *Journal of Anthropological Research* 38(2): 137–153.

BOGGS, J.

2002. "Anthropological Knowledge and Native American Cultural Practice in the Liberal Polity." *American Anthropologist* 104(2): 598–610.

BORDES, F.

1968. *The Old Stone Age.* New York: McGraw-Hill.

CHAMBERLAIN, J. G. and W. C. HARTWIG

1999. "Thomas Kuhn and Paleoanthropology." *Evolutionary Anthropology* 8(2): 42–45.

CLARK, G. A.

1993. "Paradigms in Science and Archaeology." *Journal of Archaeological Research* 1(3): 203–229.

2002. "Neandertal Archaeology: Implications for Our Origins." *American Anthropologist* 104(1): 50–67.

CLARK, G. A. and C. WILLERMET

1995. "Paradigm Crisis in Modern Human Origin Research." *Journal of Human Evolution* 29: 487–490.

CLARK, G. A. and C. WILLERMET, eds.

1997. *Conceptual Issues in Recent Modern Human Origins.* New York: Aldine de Gruyter.

CROWLEY, K.

2008. "Gameboy Havoc on LI: Teens Busted in 'Grand Theft Auto' Spree." *New York Post* (June 27, 2008). Retrieved June 9, 2009.
www.nypost.com/seven/06272008/news/regionalnews/

FREEDMAN, D.

1986. "Wife, Widow, Woman: Roles of an Anthropologist in a Transylvanian Village." In *Women in the Field* (2nd edition), edited by Peggy Golde, pp. 333–358. Berkeley, CA: University of California Press.

GOODENOUGH, W.

2002. "Anthropology in the 20th Century and Beyond." *American Anthropologist* 104(2): 423–440.

KUHN, THOMAS

1962. *The Structure of Scientific Revolutions.* Chicago, IL: University of Chicago Press.

MAYER, J.

2007. "Whatever IT Takes: The Politics of the Man behind 24." *The New Yorker* 83(1): 66–83.

MURPHY, R.

1960. *Headhunter's Heritage: Social and Economic Change among the Mundurucu Indians.* Berkeley, CA: University of California Press.

MURPHY, Y. and R. MURPHY

1985. *Women of the Forest* (2nd edition). New York: Columbia University Press.

PEACOCK, J.

1986. *The Anthropological Lens.* New York: Cambridge University Press.

SMITH, S. L. and F. B. HARROLD

1997. "A Paradigm's Worth of Difference? Understanding the Impasse over Modern Human Origins." *Yearbook of Physical Anthropology* 40: 113–138.

STUDY QUESTIONS

1. Describe this "worst case scenario": observe a car accident that two scientists also saw from the perspective of scientist one and scientist two, using as many biases as possible to show the two different "stories."

2. Two scientists—a Japanese and an American—have just discovered the bones of a 50,000-year-old human in association with flake tools. In what ways will the two scientists differ in how they go about their work because of their cultural backgrounds?

CHAPTER 8

Thinking and Acting Ethically in Anthropology

Ann Kingsolver

University of South Carolina

If you take a philosophy class on ethics, you might be discussing Jean-Paul Sartre's (1948:40) description of a student's dilemma (Should he join the resistance against fascism or continue taking care of his mother?), or you might be considering the arguments for and against euthanasia or abortion.[1] When we talk about ethics in anthropology, we narrow the scope of the questions to apply to the practice of our discipline. However, ethics always involves asking questions of yourself and others, and making decisions, usually about what will be the least harmful course of action. For example, if an archaeologist encounters human remains while digging test pits for the highway department to see whether there is any evidence of occupation by earlier groups, should the archaeologist notify someone? If so, who should be notified? Should the archaeologist continue with the excavation or stop and cover it back over, including the human remains? What laws and professional codes guide archaeologists in making such a decision? How is this an ethical problem?

What thinking anthropologically and thinking ethically have in common is this: we try to consider as many perspectives as possible with regard to whatever we are studying or whatever problems we are attempting to solve. Usually, that means actively seeking others' points of view on an issue because we cannot see all possible ramifications of an action from our own perspectives. Different cultures may have different logics, for example, when it comes to ethical decision-making, and because anthropology may involve cross-cultural communication and study, it may take teamwork to decide what would be the most beneficial process for all who might be affected by anthropological research. Asking questions is a very important, active part of acting ethically in anthropology. Rather than simply learning a list of "dos and don'ts" in the discipline, anthropological ethics involves learning how to ask questions that are well informed by past experiences, professional guidelines, and the laws, policies, and cultural preferences of those in whose regions we work. As a student of anthropology, you not only have a responsibility to think and act ethically along with the professionals, you also have rights as specified in the American Anthropological Association's Code of Ethics.

In this chapter, I will talk about why ethics matter in anthropology, including ethics in the classroom. I will provide examples of the way anthropologists keep learning from our mistakes, creating and revising ethical codes that are meant to guide (but are unable to sanction) behavior by fellow anthropologists. Specific topics addressed in courses on anthropological ethics that will be summarized briefly in this chapter include informed consent; human rights; cultural and ethical relativism; the U.S. Native American Graves Protection and Repatriation Act (**NAGPRA**) of 1990; intellectual, biological, and other property rights; whistle-blowing; ethical issues in the collection and representation of data; visual ethics; insider and outsider research issues; equity issues inside and outside universities; conflicts in **accountability**; and collaborative decision-making.

Anthropological learning implies contracts of *respect* on several levels. Professional anthropologists, whether working in academic or other contexts, are bound by personal and professional ethics to respect those with whom they work, living or dead, at home (wherever home may be) or in another region. In turn, as you learn about the cultural, linguistic, biological, historical, and prehistoric aspects of human experience from what professional anthropologists (including archaeologists) are learning, you enter into that contract of respect as well. For example, if you see a film in class that was made by an anthropologist, the practice of professional ethics means that the maker of that film obtained (or should have obtained) the consent of those being filmed to have their images and words studied by you and others. When consent is negotiated, as I will explain later in this chapter, the anthropologist explains the project as fully as possible. The agreement made between the filmmaker and those filmed is entered into, by extension, by the person showing you the film and by you, the viewer. As an undergraduate, then, you are acting as a professional anthropologist when you view a film with respect for those portrayed, no matter how different their life experience may be from your own.

As a student of anthropology, you need to follow not only any ethical codes for students on your campus, but also any national regulations that may pertain to student researchers. For example, in the United States, on campuses and in communities, there are Institutional Review Boards made up of people from various backgrounds who review research proposals and classroom exercises that involve human subjects and decide whether they might cause harm to those being asked to participate in the research. If you are conducting a life history interview or taping and transcribing a conversation, you should give the person you interview a description of your project and contact information and obtain his or her consent before you begin the interview. *Informed consent* means that a person knows as much as he or she can about the purpose of the research project in which he or she agrees to participate, the methods used, and the dissemination of results, and agrees to work with the researcher by voluntarily signing a consent form or giving verbal consent on an audiotape or videotape. The researcher is responsible for explaining the project clearly, respecting the collaborator's (a name for the person agreeing to participate in the research) wishes regarding anonymity or other stipulations, and providing the person who is helping or teaching the anthropologist with the results of the project. You can find guidelines for informed consent, and the entire Code of Ethics, on the American Anthropological Association's Web site (http://aaanet.org).

One basic ethical guideline to remember is that whereas journalists are accountable to the public (providing the full story), anthropologists are accountable to those from whom we request time and knowledge. This may sometimes mean that the ethical thing to do is to *not* tell the full story. For example, if naming ancestors is culturally forbidden and documenting a family history violates the contract of respect an anthropologist has with his or her collaborators, then the kinship chart should be left out of the publication. Sometimes anthropologists find themselves with unanticipated ethical dilemmas. What if a person being interviewed mentions having engaged in an illegal activity? Are fieldnotes private or public? What if an ethnographer's work is used by a political faction to justify violent acts? Can an anthropologist really say that he or she can foresee no harmful effects of publishing (or not publishing) research results?

Not too many years ago, as I was driving down a highway, I saw a billboard in front of a church that was advertising the title of the sermon for the following Sunday. It read, "The Evil in Cultural Relativism." I bring this up here to explain that in anthropology, cultural relativism does not mean "anything goes," which is probably how the phrase was used in the Christian sermon. To anthropologists, cultural relativism means that we (going back to Franz Boas, at the beginning of the twentieth century) endeavor to understand a culture by its own logic or rules rather than our own (if they are different). This does not mean that we personally agree with every practice we study as anthropologists. **Ethical relativism**, in which a person suspends judgment on cultural practices and believes they are all equally valid, is separate from **cultural relativism**, in which a culture is not judged as good or bad but is understood using its own framework.[2] For example, an anthropologist may be observing cultural relativism to understand the practice of infanticide as it is explained by a practitioner and at the same time have a personal belief that infanticide violates **human rights**. Anthropologists come from many different cultural and religious backgrounds, and have very different views on such questions as when human life begins and ends or whether female circumcision is a cultural right or a violation of a human right. There are ongoing debates about such issues at professional anthropology meetings, and anthropologists participate in United Nations' conversations on international human rights. You might find it interesting to read the United Nations Universal Declaration of Human Rights,[3] which was signed in 1948 by representatives of 48 countries, including the United States. People in many current social movements are asking their own countries to observe this document, and it outlines the larger contract of respect within which we think and act as anthropologists.

In the past, some anthropologists have made what they thought at the time were ethical decisions that have been seen as unethical by others at the time or later, or that the anthropologists themselves came to view later as unethical. Because ethical decisions are context-dependent, views on how one should behave ethically can change. For example, several famous U.S. anthropologists provided information about Pacific cultures in their work for the U.S. Office of Strategic Services (or military intelligence) during World War II, believing it to be the right way to use their professional knowledge for their country.[4] A few anthropologists worked for the Central Intelligence Agency during the Vietnam War. That brought outcries from other anthropologists, who did not want the discipline to be associated with spying because anthropologists' role as cultural observers can be uncomfortably confused with that "spy" role anyway. Renewed debates about anthropologists' work with the U.S. military, and other contractors, were reflected in the 2009 revision of the American Anthropological Association's Code of Ethics (www.aaanet.org/issues/policy-advocacy/Code-of-Ethics.cfm), which states that clandestine research violates anthropological research ethics. The ethical issue here is related to *conflicts in accountability*. Were anthropologists who were working for the government during World War II working to promote anthropological understanding or to promote their government's ability to undermine another government? In a very different example of conflicting accountability, if an anthropologist is hired by a government to assess a social services program, is he or she working for the government or for the program?

You can learn more about the history of anthropology and how we have, we hope, learned from our experiences in the discipline by reading the collections edited by Carolyn Fluehr-Lobban (2003) and Walter Goldschmidt (1979). Fluehr-Lobban discusses how anthropologists have drafted and redrafted ethical codes to reflect contemporary views, and she provides examples of them over time. One ethical controversy in anthropology that you might look into is the accusation by a journalist that several anthropologists acted unethically in their research among the Yanomami people in the Amazon region. Although the ethical codes of the discipline of anthropology were reassessed in view of this controversy, our professional organizations do not grant and remove licenses, as is the case with doctors and lawyers. Any charges arising from such controversies go through legal systems in the relevant countries. **Whistle-blowing**, or speaking up about perceived ethical and legal violations even when it puts one at risk of losing one's job or worse, involves ethical decision-making and a need for legislative and professional protection. On the other hand, of course, the power of labeling someone as unethical brings up its own ethical (and legal) problems. What are the ethical responsibilities of anthropologists regarding passing along information (a charge of ethical misconduct, for example) about which they have no direct knowledge? One of our responsibilities is to be familiar with professional guidelines and to know how to find sources and procedures for ethical decision-making and conflict resolution rather than ignoring issues raised. In the future, indigenous nations and other polities will be making the guidelines for anthropological research permission much more distinct, whether anthropologists are "insiders" or "outsiders."

I have discussed your *responsibilities* as a student of anthropology to think ethically; what about your *rights*? The Code of Ethics approved in 1998 and then in 2009 by the American Anthropological Association includes a section on the ethical responsibilities of anthropologists to students, including not discriminating "on the basis of sex, marital status, 'race,' social class, political convictions, disability, religion, ethnic background, national origin, sexual orientation, age, or other criteria irrelevant to academic performance." Sexual harassment and other abuses of power are forbidden by U.S. anthropologists' professional code and by legal codes that pertain to your institution of learning. Additionally, anthropologists who teach and belong to the American Anthropological Association are bound by its Code of Ethics to be available to students, counsel students about career opportunities, assist them in finding professional positions, and give fair credit and compensation for participation in their research.

Giving *credit* and *compensation* to anyone involved in anthropological research is an important ethical principle. This is an area of much discussion in the discipline. Should all anthropological work be coauthored by anthropologists and their collaborators? How is a shaman's knowledge of plant uses, for example, protected legally and in ethical codes as intellectual property, and how should an ethnobotanist compensate the individual or group for reproducing that knowledge? What if the information could be used by pharmaceutical companies to make a profit if an anthropologist published it? Indigenous activists have been working to secure intellectual property rights, and there are sources that anthropologists with ethical dilemmas can consult.[5]

Most professional anthropologists are working in occupations other than teaching, and so our ethical codes extend beyond the classroom. The first professional code for anthropologists in the United States was the Code of Ethics composed by a committee of the Society of Applied Anthropology in 1949. Margaret Mead chaired that committee, and the code was intended

> to advance those forms of human relationships which contribute to the integrity of the individual human being; to maintain scientific and professional integrity and responsibility without fear or favor to the limit of the foreseeable effects of their actions; to respect both human personality and cultural values; to publish and share new discoveries and methods with colleagues; those are the principles which should be accepted and which should be known to be accepted by all those who work in the disciplines affecting human relationships.[6]

More than 50 years later, anthropologists find that there are many more specific guidelines, usually legal codes, governing work both inside and outside of academia. The NAGPRA of 1990, for example, has had a profound effect on the practice of archaeology, biological anthropology, and museum anthropology. Skeletal remains identified as Native American were required by an act of Congress to be *repatriated* (returned) to Native American nations (and some groups such as the Lakota volunteered to repatriate remains of those unidentified by a specific nation) for *reburial* according to their custom. Because having skeletal remains of ancestors, sometimes obtained through violence or theft, on display violated most cultural customs, NAGPRA specified not only full **repatriation** by a deadline (now past) but also new guidelines for what to do when potential Native American remains are encountered during an archaeological excavation.

Native American nations have specified which individuals can oversee decision-making and reburial as such situations arise. The response of the anthropological community to NAGPRA was not a simple one; some considered the reburial of collections to be a loss of potentially helpful scholarship. In some cases, there were collaborations between skeletal biological anthropologists, archaeologists, and Native American nations to learn what they could about the health and lifeways of the ancestors whose remains were in research collections before they were repatriated. Educational programs were established to share those results with those whose ancestors were reburied.

Anthropologists have an ethical obligation to share what we learn from our research and to do so honestly. What does that mean? You probably learned about plagiarism through student codes at your school, but beyond plagiarism, there are other ways of being dishonest in reporting what we learn. What if a linguistic anthropologist uses a single example as representative of a shift in language practices without reporting the sample size? What if a map is drawn using a scale that misrepresents results? How can census figures be used properly? There are many ethical questions that arise in the collection and representation of data. For this reason, most of the information presented to you in class has gone through a process called **peer review** or *intersubjective agreement,* in which a number of scholars agree that an article or book may be published because it represents a clear and current understanding of an aspect of anthropological knowledge.

How do anthropologists decide what is reliable information? This has changed over the decades. One example is the *insider/outsider debate* and the discussion of *objectivity.* Early in the history of the discipline, as anthropologists drew on the empirical tradition of the natural sciences to help form the methods of a new field of knowledge, "objectivity" was taken to mean the clarity of vision one can have through being an outside, or impartial, observer. Over time, anthropologists saw that their discipline is more complicated than that. We are not observing another species through a microscope; anthropologists are always humans learning about humanity from humans, and that puts us squarely into the picture, whether we admit it or not. Generations of feminist and postcolonial anthropologists introduced a new meaning of "objectivity" into the discipline including multiple perspectives and making our own anthropological position explicit. The gender, native language, age, or nationality of the researcher may make a difference in what questions are asked and how they are answered. Whether to consider insider or outsider knowledge as more reliable continues to be a debate in the discipline, but most of us find we are a bit of both (insider and outsider) in any particular research context. Ethical questions here have to do with how we consider the research enterprise. For example, are those interviewed accorded rights as co-constructors of anthropological knowledge? For example, does being an insider or outsider make a difference regarding the maintenance or disruption of stereotypes?

Visual ethics is a whole area of anthropological discussion currently under construction. Perhaps you will contribute to this discussion. It is possible to obtain informed consent when photographing an individual, but what is the best way to obtain permission in large group settings, if they are not public events? Are the photographs or film footage taken by anthropologists (including anthropology students) the intellectual property of the photographers or the property of the subjects of the images? Some anthropologists, on the consent form, give a date by which the people photographed may withdraw their consent. Anthropologists often provide an opportunity for the people filmed to view and comment on the film in a public venue and are ethically obligated to provide copies of images to those photographed. Given what was said earlier about the context-dependent nature of anthropological ethics, what do you think should be done about photographs and films made before informed consent became the practice? Should descendants be compensated for the use of their ancestors' images? Should these ethnographic materials no longer be available for public viewing?

There are many other ethical questions for students of anthropology to ask, and new ones are constantly arising as well. What does the Internet mean for the dissemination of images and research findings? How has the discipline both supported and challenged racism and eugenicist policy over the last century and a half? Is there a collaborative research process that can be relied upon to "keep us honest" in our research?

I hope that you can see, through the topics introduced in this chapter, that the discipline of anthropology has not made a steady progression from unethical to ethical practice, or the reverse, but as a community of researchers, teachers, students, and practitioners, we constantly ask questions and often have disagreements about the most beneficial ways to proceed with our work as anthropologists. I encourage you to look at the Code of Ethics on the American Anthropological Association Web site, such as NAGPRA, and to ask yourself as you learn about the range of human experiences through anthropology course work how you are related to those you study and learn from through a contract of respect. Thinking anthropologically means thinking ethically as well.

NOTES

1. I thank F. Michael McLain, my philosophical ethics professor two decades ago, for helping me locate the Sartre reference.
2. For a discussion of cultural, ethical, and epistemological relativism, see Whitaker (1996).
3. This Declaration of Human Rights may be found at http://un.org/en/documents/udhr.
4. For further information, see Alcalay (1992).
5. The United Nations Declaration on the Rights of Indigenous Peoples (www.un.org/esa/socdev/unpfii/en/declaration.html), for example, was approved in 2007.
6. This code is Appendix A in Fluehr-Lobban (2003).

REFERENCES

ALCALAY, G.

1992. "The United States Anthropologist in Micronesia: Towards a Counter-hegemonic Study of *Sapiens*." In *Confronting the Margaret Mead Legacy: Scholarship, Empire, and the South Pacific,* edited by L. Foerstel and A. Gilliam, pp. 173–203. Philadelphia: Temple University Press.

FLUEHR-LOBBAN, C., ed.

1991. *Ethics and the Profession of Anthropology: Dialogue for a New Era.* Philadelphia: University of Pennsylvania Press.

GOLDSCHMIDT, W., ed.

1979. *The Uses of Anthropology.* Washington, DC: American Anthropological Association.

SARTRE, J. P.

1948. *Existentialism and Humanism* (P. Mairet, trans.). London, UK: Methuen.

WHITAKER, M. P.

1996. "Relativism." In *Encyclopedia of Social and Cultural Anthropology,* edited by A. Barnard and J. Spencer, pp. 478–482. New York: Routledge.

STUDY QUESTIONS

1. As a cultural anthropologist about to take a group of students who have never been away from home to the New Guinea highlands, what ethical responsibilities will you tell them about and expect them to adhere to while there?
2. You are an archaeologist and have just found what appear to be human bones near an American Indian reservation. What do you do next and why?

CHAPTER 9

Applying Anthropological Knowledge

Aaron Podolefsky
Central Missouri State University

> I would like to try an experiment. Before you go on to the next paragraph, look up from the page—close your eyes if you must—and ask yourself, "What are the three or four greatest problems facing America or the world today?" Take a few minutes to think about it. Jot them down on a piece of paper.

I have asked this question on the first day of my introductory anthropology classes for most of my career. Students take a few moments to think about the question; then, if I do not rush to fill in the silence, a few venture their opinions. As students share their short lists with each other, general discussion turns to those things that are repeated on the majority of lists.

Students' concerns have changed somewhat over the years, but most themes have remained reasonably constant. Students see our biggest problems as crime, poverty, environmental issues, malnutrition and starvation (in the Third World), war, discrimination, unemployment, AIDS, economic development, the global economy, or changing values (or unchanging values, depending on one's view). Today I expect the economy and unemployment, sustainability, and terrorism or bioterrorism to be high on students' lists, as might be ethics. How does your list compare?

Conspicuously absent are such things like how to make a faster computer, how to make cars more comfortable, how to make sure cell phones reach us while backpacking, or other concerns that intrude into our daily lives.

What students find interesting is that the most frequently mentioned problems are social problems or have significant social dimensions. Class discussions

76

usually lead to students' realization that even problems that do not seem to be social in nature, such as sustainability, have roots in social behavior. It soon becomes clear that the means for resolving these problems probably also involve changes in social behavior or social policy. It seems odd to me that this comes as such a surprise to so many.

Anthropologists often apply their knowledge and ways of thinking to questions like these (Podolefsky and Brown 2007). Addressing questions that have a direct impact on individuals' lives or affect society through changing social policies is what I call **applying anthropology**. Worded differently, applying anthropology involves using knowledge, methods, and anthropological ways of thinking to examine problems and issues of contemporary concern and to bring about change. This is a bit broader than the subfield of anthropology called applied anthropology. From this broader point of view, you can apply anthropological thinking in fields ranging from business (Janus 1983; Labs 1992; Reeves-Ellington 1993) to engineering, as in the development of crash dummies and ergonomic design (designing things so that people and things interact most efficiently and safely) (Hertzberg 1979).

Distinguishing the application of a body of knowledge or methods from research into everyday questions is not unique to anthropology. Scientific work often is classified as basic research, applied research, and development. The distinctions are a bit fuzzy, but, as with most aspects of language, separating the concepts helps us think about the differences.

Basic research includes studies conducted to discover knowledge for its own sake. Investigation takes place without particular regard for a topic's practical importance or impact. In the end, of course, basic research creates knowledge that forms the foundation for understanding and enables researchers to think about practical problems in new ways.

Applied research differs in that it examines problems that have a directly practical outcome. Anthropologists who apply anthropology may work for clients who want to learn fairly specific things. For example, medical examiners may engage biological anthropologists to help them identify long-buried bones that might be the remains of a missing person. Given their expertise, biological anthropologists are able to make estimates about the height, sex, and "race," of the victim of a crime and, by applying their skills, help identify the person (Snow and Luke 1970). Anthropologists have worked on cases involving individual remains, airplane disasters, and mass grave sites (American Anthropological Association 1982; Huyghe 1988).

Applied research may also examine questions that are more sweeping. Some of my own work has involved community crime prevention policy (Podolefsky 1983; Podolefsky and DuBow 1981). Although my earlier work focused on New Guinea highlands law, I was readily able to apply anthropological theories and methods to urban American settings. Applied anthropologists may use their knowledge and methods to assess policies and practices that can have significant impact.

Development is the use of knowledge derived from both basic and applied research to create (develop) approaches to solving practical problems. Archaeologists Alan Kolata and Oswaldo Rivera were excavating in Bolivia when they recognized that prehistoric societies had used extensive irrigation canal systems to enhance crop growth. When the Spaniards came to South America, they brought their own "hacienda" system, which replaced the native "raised fields" system. The new system did not work very well in the high Andes. Kolata and Oswaldo enticed several local farmers to experiment with the old system, and the crop yield increased by 20 percent. Reintroducing this farming method was so successful that the Bolivian government sponsored teaching the technique to local farmers to reduce the region's nutritional problems (Straughan 1991).

It is not how one thinks but what one thinks about that distinguishes applied anthropological thinking from other types of anthropological thinking. For students, applying anthropology means using its intellectual tools to think about contemporary concerns at home and abroad. Applying anthropological thinking takes advantage of the fundamental knowledge generated through basic research, uses the methods and theories of basic research, and maintains the standards for explanation that apply to basic research. It follows that the nature of the thinking, in most respects, used to apply anthropology is very similar to the thinking strategies described in previous chapters.

How do you approach and think about critical social questions? Do you think about the connections within a social system?

What if we asked questions about the simplest of things. For example, what was the effect of the introduction of air-conditioning? That's easy. Everyone got cooler. True, but what else? When I was young (in the 1950s), before air-conditioning was widespread, my grandparents spent hot New York City summer nights sitting with their neighbors on the steps outside their apartment building. Often the men played cards and the women played Mahjong until the apartments cooled off. Everyone knew everyone else, which led to social cohesion and mutual aid in difficult times. Today, the apartments are air-conditioned, people do not congregate outside where it is cooler, and people in that same neighborhood hardly know their neighbors. Streets at night are occupied mostly by youths, and there is little supervision. Crime can occur with few to observe. Maybe air-conditioning caused abandoned streets, which caused the increase in crime? Well, let's not go that far. But you can see that by looking at a common situation that occurred all over the country, one can speculate about a range of social consequences. So what might happen to a small South American community when television is introduced? (See Pace 1993). Or cell phones?

I believe that most people do not recognize social and cultural complexity. Because we all live within a society, it is intimately familiar. Everyday circumstances (or even rare events such as the introduction of air-conditioning) do not call out for explanation. Rather, they simply are the way it is. This is not the case with all academic fields.

As an undergraduate, I earned a degree in mathematics, but friends never asked about mathematics. Odd as it may seem, I was intrigued by a number sequence called Fibonacci numbers. Outside a small group of classmates, no one was interested in talking about Fibonacci or the many computer applications. I never attended a party where someone struck up a conversation on any mathematically related topic. The reason was very clear: few people consider themselves sufficiently expert to discuss these complex problems (not to mention that it is boring to most folks). Everyone knows that special knowledge is needed to venture a rational opinion.

I had just the opposite experience in the social sciences, particularly when I was researching urban crime. For example, I will bet that most of you had an opinion about whether air-conditioning caused urban crime, but none ventured an opinion on Mr. Fibonacci.

People, society, and culture are familiar; we are enveloped in society in our everyday existence. This proximity leads people to believe they understand how society works, how it came to be the way it is, and how its institutions function. Everyone is an expert on culture, or so they think, but few see the complexity of social issues or even the potential for the link between factors that are not apparently related (air-conditioning and crime). Commonly, people form opinions with no knowledge of social theory, evidentiary data, or comparison cases. This has long been a frustration to me, but it has grown worse in recent years. It seems more common these days to assert that one's opinion is one's own, and because it is "my opinion," it should not be subject to scrutiny by others because an opinion is an opinion and all opinions are equal. What is worse, people often don't really scrutinize their own opinions.

Don't get me wrong. People have a right to their opinions. And I strongly advocate students having many passionate views. The function of education, of course, is to help you learn how to turn your and other opinions into suppositions (if not testable hypotheses) and to explore the validity of these suppositions.

It seems that because the questions, concerns, or problems of social sciences are commonplace, some assume that the answers or solutions must be simple or obvious. Ask anyone how to reduce crime in this country, and you will probably get a strongly held opinion. Some will suggest longer jail terms, others reducing poverty, still others less violent television, and so it goes. One needs to ask, "How would I know? Are there data?"

Anthropology has some conspicuous advantages for helping students learn to think scientifically about social problems. It also has some disadvantages, but these can easily be overcome. Both the advantages and disadvantages result from anthropology's exotic nature. Unlike most other social sciences, anthropology's subject matter is unfamiliar. Unlike sociology and psychology, human evolution and archaeology are not part of our daily lives, and few students have spent much time in the far-off corners of the globe where most cultural anthropological field research is conducted.

The downside is that the exotic nature of life in Fiji, South Africa, or New Guinea can lead to a fascination with facts and descriptions rather than explanations. There is nothing wrong with a fascination about what people eat, how many husbands or wives they can marry, how they wage warfare, or descriptions of their religious lives. But we must go beyond mere description.

The upside to this unfamiliarity—the anthropological advantage—is that students encounter a wide variety of social arrangements that beg to be explained. Once one has read and understood the description of a place, people, or social situation, the student's challenge is to remember to ask the question "why." For example, one could read about the status of women in one or more societies and stop there. Or one could ask, "Why do women have equal status in some societies and not in others?" Or one could hypothesize that inequality is most common where women are economically dependent, and equality is most common where women are economically independent (Friedl 1978). Then one might ask, "If women's status is related to access to the economy, how might equality be fostered?"

In this example, the last of these questions applies the knowledge of the first two to the solution of a practical problem. A possible solution might be to provide interest-free small business loans to women. This might work well in one setting, but what about doing this in India, for example? What might be the cultural impediments? What values, beliefs, and structures would have to be overcome for this to be successful? What are the roles of women in this society? Anthropologists have tackled these questions.

We apply anthropological thinking to questions that come to us because of our own interest or because others need to know answers. Policy makers may want to know how best to implement a local economic development program (Murray 1987) or how best to reduce the refuse in landfills (Harrison, Rathje, and Hughes 1975). Corporate executives may want to know how to understand another culture so that their managers can best work with managers from this culture (Reeves-Ellington 1993). There may be differences ranging from beliefs and values to how organizations are structured. Managers may want to know how to prepare their employees or their family to live in another country (Trager 1987). Physicians or social service workers may need to know how to interact with new immigrants from other countries (Johnson 1991).

In each of these cases and many others that could be cited, it is important that someone first recognize these as issues or problems. The difficulties encountered by spouses of employees who are stationed overseas were long ignored, but ignoring the problem clearly led to low productivity. Why did this take so long to recognize?

Once such issues are recognized, people need to decide whether it is a problem that needs to be solved. There is an important but seldom recognized difference between *issues* and *problems*. An issue is something that well-informed people will disagree about. A problem is a condition that everyone agrees is unacceptable. We should recognize the difference and not be surprised that it is more difficult to resolve issues.

Let's look for a moment at the question of women's access to family planning information and birth control in Third World countries (Schuler and Hashemi 1995). Is this an issue to be resolved or a problem to be solved? It is clear that in cases in which a nation's population growth is staggering and malnutrition is common, agreement can be reached on the goal of reducing population growth. But decisions about how to reach this goal may be more difficult because it may be framed in terms of values. Once the decisions are made, the problem becomes how best to communicate family planning information. It turns out that this and similar efforts are much more difficult to achieve than it seems on its face.

Too often policy makers develop plans and programs but do not assess their effectiveness. In our family planning example, there are two goal levels. Once a program is designed, does it, in fact, disseminate the family planning information, and does it lead to lower rates of childbirth? How do we know? This is one of the major questions for evaluation research. It is enough here to point out that evaluating programs is a great way to test our understanding of society. Programs based on a sound analysis of the cause of a phenomenon, if well implemented, should be more successful than those that were based on poor theory.

Because cultural anthropologists have worked in so many different cultures, they have become sensitive to how *categories* are defined and how things are *counted.* It is a perspective that greatly respects an insider or native view of the world. What is a crime, for example? Or what constitutes divorce in a particular culture? Anthropologists, and other social scientists as well, sometimes run into difficulties because the words we use have common meanings that can create confusion. This happened to me as I was preparing for field research in the Papua New Guinea highlands. There was considerable disagreement about whether there was "law" in New Guinea. In 1958, Leopold Pospisil wrote that if he adopted a common anthropological definition, the systematic application of force, he would have reported that the Kapauku had no law. Klaus Koch (1970; 1974) studied warfare and concluded that military operations indicate the absence, inadequacy, or breakdown of other mechanisms, such as law, designed to reduce conflict. And Hatanaka (1973) reported that "the developed concept of 'law' and related notions are not easily applicable to activities in the traditional societies of New Guinea. There is a virtual absence of authority, leadership, and law as usually understood." These anthropologists had differing opinions on whether New Guinea societies have law.

How, I wondered, could densely populated tribes of thousands of people live together without law? I decided that worrying about the definition was limiting my thinking. I decided to investigate what people did when they had grievances. I found ample opportunity for research and discovered that highlanders have a variety of two-party and three-party strategies for conflict resolution that fit the needs of their culture and society (Podolefsky 1992).

Anthropological thinking is a habit of mind that begins by questioning fundamental categories of meaning. It questions what things are lumped together and therefore asks fundamental questions about quantitative data. I was fascinated by a study that showed that what had been thought to be a steady rise in child abuse over a number of years turned out to be the result of changing definitions of child abuse, which resulted in an increase in instances that were counted. Similarly, in my study of urban crime prevention, I pointed out that programs that urge citizens to report crimes can cause the crime rate to go up because the crime rate is based on the count of reported crimes, not the actual number of crimes (which is unknown because many are not reported). Thus, a successful block watch program may cause the official crime rate to go up. Such modest complexities suggest that thinking anthropologically, especially where conclusions can have critical public policy consequences, requires us to look beyond the obvious into the social construction of data and social categories.

CONCLUSION

No matter where we look around us, from Africa to the Middle East to our own nation, state, town, and neighborhood, there are complex and critically important issues that deserve our attention. Some are global policy issues that may affect the lives of millions of people. Others are local questions, such as whether a social program actually achieved its goal. What these have in common is that thinking about either requires habits of mind that allow people to see below the surface to the underlying themes of human behavior.

To apply anthropological knowledge, one must recognize patterns that lead to the application of theory and the generation of hypotheses. One must know how to collect data of various kinds and how to roll those data up into an understanding that goes beyond the mere summary of numeric or descriptive information.

What may be most important for you to know is that this intellectual ability does not come instantaneously. Academic skills and abilities come no easier than athletic skills. We know that a great swimmer or diver must practice hours each day. And so it is with the ability to apply anthropological thinking. Seek out opportunities. When you read a news article about a nation in which women are not allowed to drive, go beyond merely saying, "Oh, that's their custom" or "Gee, that's not fair." Ask yourself, for example, how this affects women's role in the family and in society. Ask yourself about the function of this custom for maintaining the social order (equality or inequality). Ask yourself how this social custom reinforces other social institutions such as religious and political practices. Ask yourself who benefits and who loses. And if you want to apply your thinking to creating change, ask yourself who will object if those women drive and how the change you seek will affect other aspects of society and culture.

Applying anthropological thinking to complex issues takes incisive, penetrating, and rigorous thinking. Apply this standard to your thinking about other peoples and cultures. Then look in the mirror and apply it to your own.

REFERENCES

American Anthropological Association
   1982. "American Anthropological Association 1982 profile." *Anthropology Newsletter* 23–26.
Friedl, E.
   1978. "Society and Sex Roles." *Human Nature* (April): 31–35.
Harrison, G. G., W. L. Rathje, and W. W. Hughes
   1975. "Food Waste Behavior in an Urban Population." *Journal of Nutrition Education* 7(1): 13–16.

HATANAKA, S.
1973. "Conflict of Law in a New Guinea Highland Society." *Man* 8: 59–73.
HERTZBERG, H. T. E.
1979. "Engineering Anthropology: Past, Present, and Potential." In *The Uses of Anthropology*, edited by W. Goldschmidt. Washington, DC: American Anthropological Association.
HUYGHE, P.
1988. "No Bone Unturned." *Discover* 9(12): 38–45.
JANUS, N.
1983. "Advertising and Global Culture." *Cultural Survival* 7(2): 28–31.
JOHNSON, T. M.
1991. "Anthropology and the World of Physicians." *Anthropology Newsletter*, in Podolefsky and Brown (2002): 271–274, November/December.
KOCH, K.
1970. "Warfare and Anthrophagy in Jale Society." *Ibijdragen tot de taal-, Land- en Volkenkunde* 126: 37–58.
1974. *War and Peace in Jalimo.* Cambridge, MA: Harvard University Press.
LABS, J.
1992. "Corporate Anthropologists." *Personnel Journal* 71(1): 81–87.
MURRAY, G. F.
1987. "The Domestication of Wood in Haiti: A Case Study in Applied Evolution." In *Anthropological Praxis*, edited by R. M. Wulff and S. J. Fiske. Boulder, CO: Westview Press.
PACE, R.
1993. "First-Time Televiewing in Amazonia." *Ethnology* 32(2): 187–205.
PODOLEFSKY, A.
1983. *Case Studies in Community Crime Prevention.* Springfield, IL: Charles C. Thomas.
1992. *Simbu Law.* New York: Harcourt Brace Jovanovich.
PODOLEFSKY, A. and P. J. BROWN
2007. *Applying Anthropology: An Introductory Reader* (8th edition). New York: McGraw-Hill.
PODOLEFSKY, A. and F. DuBOW
1981. *Strategies for Community Crime Prevention: Collective Responses to Crime in Urban America.* Springfield, IL: Charles C. Thomas.
POSPISIL, L.
1958. *Kapauku Papuans and Their Law.* New Haven, CT: Yale University Press.
REEVES-ELLINGTON, R. H.
1993. "Using Cultural Skills for Cooperative Advantage in Japan." *Human Organization* 52(2): 203–215.
SCHULER, S. R. and S. M. HASHEMI
1995. "Family Planning Outreach and Credit Programs in Rural Bangladesh." *Human Organization* 54(4): 455–461.
SNOW, C. and J. L. LUKE
1970. "The Oklahoma City Child Disappearances of 1967: Forensic Anthropology in the Identification of Skeletal Remains." *Journal of Forensic Sciences* 15(2): 125–153.

STRAUGHAN, B.
   1991. "The Secrets of Ancient Tiwanaku Are Benefiting Today's Bolivia." *Smithsonian* 21(11): 38–47.
TRAGER, L.
   1987. "Living Abroad: Cross-Cultural Training for Families." *Practicing Anthropology* 9(3): 5–11.

STUDY QUESTIONS

1. Given the definition of applied anthropology, why isn't excavation (archaeological and bioanthropological) applied anthropology? Could they be?
2. Describe either the original research done in New Guinea by the author or the work by Alan Kolata in South America, and given the definition of applied anthropology, describe what the expert is attempting to do and why it is applied anthropology.

CHAPTER 10

Making Ideas Researchable[1]

Philip Carl Salzman
McGill University

Patricia C. Rice
West Virginia University

In our everyday conversation, as well as in discussions of anthropology, we often use general ideas—such as university, intelligence, democracy, kinship, "race," civilization, equality, and urban life—which are pretty abstract and not so easy to define. Is "kinship" a "blood tie"? Is "democracy" collective decision-making by all citizens? Is "race" a biological group? Does "equality" mean everyone is the same in every characteristic? The definitions of these and similar ideas and concepts have been the subjects of debate by philosophers, social and biological scientists, and citizens through the ages, and continue to be debated. Perhaps a final resolution is impossible, and even undesirable; but each discussion and each research effort requires at least a working definition, so that we know what we are talking about and what we are looking for.

Even when we succeed in stretching our brains and agreeing on a definition, it is commonly difficult to establish whether a particular quality, event, place, or population in the real world is an example of the general idea we have defined. Does Ottawa have urban life? Are Jews a "race"? Is there equality in the United States? Do the Caribbean Islands constitute a civilization? To decide the answers to these questions, our definitions have to be supplemented with criteria to help us judge whether specific cases are examples of the definition in question. For example, looking at equality in industrial societies, if we have defined equality as everyone being the same, we would want to look at the following: (1) Do all people have the same level of material wealth? (2) Do all citizens have the same legal rights? (3) Do all citizens have equal say in political decisions?

Making general ideas and concepts specific and definite, both in their meaning and in their applicability, is a central part of thinking anthropologically. We can only begin to engage in anthropological research when we have clarified the meanings of our research ideas and concepts, and figured out how to tell whether the people and places, processes, and characteristics that we observe are or are not instances of these ideas and concepts. So, before we begin research, we have to define our ideas clearly to make them specific and precise, and we must develop specific criteria for deciding whether any specific case, either activity or feature, is an example of the idea or concept.

SPECIFYING NOMADISM

To illustrate, let us begin with a relatively simple example, a concept mentioned in Chapter 2: nomadism. As with all concepts, "nomadism" can be, and has been, defined in various ways: "wandering," "full time movement," "movement of the household as part of making a living." I prefer the latter definition, because "wandering" suggests aimlessness, which is far from the reality of nomadic life, and because "full time movement" could describe tourists and traveling salesmen who leave their families behind in stationary residences. "Movement of the household as part of making a living" is still a broad definition of nomadism, because it could include one or a few households, rather than an entire community or society, as in migrant laborers, just as it could be used to designate an entire community or society.

What criteria can we use to tell whether particular individuals are or are not nomads (according to the definition we have chosen above)?

- One criterion is whether the individual is moving much of the time rather than remaining stationary. We could decide, for example, to count as "nomadic" someone who spends no more than 3 months in one locality.
- A second criterion would be whether or not the individual is moving with or without the other members of his or her household. If the person is unmarried, then we would ask if he or she is traveling with his or her mother or father. If the person is married, we would ask whether she or he is traveling with her or his spouse and children (if any).
- A third criterion would be whether or not the purpose of movement is making a living. Is the person traveling to find game or wild plants, and thus making a living as a nomadic hunter–gatherer? Or is the purpose to move the livestock to better pasture and water sources, and thus making a living as a nomadic pastoralist? Or is the purpose to find work as a paid hand, and thus making a living as a migrant laborer?

The definition and related criteria allow us to establish whether a particular individual is or is not nomadic. Further criteria would be required to decide whether a larger unit, beyond the household, such as the community or society, is or is not nomadic. We might, for example, decide to establish a criterion such as the percentage of nomads in a community or society that is required before we would characterize or label it as "nomadic." We could say that 60 percent of the members of a community or society must be nomadic before it could be called a nomadic community or society. By this criterion, villages in Rajasthan, India, which have around 5 to 20 percent nomadic pastoralists, could not be considered nomadic communities. But tribes in Baluchistan, Iran, in which 80 percent of members are nomadic, could be considered nomadic tribes.

What we have done here, to make the concept of "nomadism" researchable, is to select one of many possible definitions, and to specify a series of criteria to allow us to judge if any particular individual is nomadic by our definition. As well, we have developed criteria to tell us whether a community or larger society could be considered nomadic. Having done this, we are in a position to begin research on particular people and larger populations on the subject of nomadism.

SPECIFYING THE NEOLITHIC

The original definition of the Neolithic (literally "The New Stone Age") was made by John Lubbock in 1865. He defined it as the cultural period when humans began to cultivate plants and keep domestic animals but still used stone tools (as opposed to metal tools). He used 2 criteria: **domestication** and stone tools. Other definitions followed, including:

- the use of ground stone tools;
- a phase of human cultural development marked mainly by village settlement, domestication, and new implement types of flaked and ground stone tools;
- symptomized by pottery, **sedentism**, and villages; and
- a period of polished stone axes.

These definitions come from post-2000 archaeology/prehistory encyclopedias and textbooks; note the criteria additions of specific tool changes, sedentism, pottery, and villages.

Defining the Neolithic in prehistory has chronological overtones because as archaeologists found evidence for domestication of plants/animals, and ground/polished stone tools, or pottery, or sedentism, or villages in more than one place and time, the definition changed.

As of now, it seems best to define the Neolithic as a cultural period where domestication of plants and/or animals occurred. Although the term Neolithic implies new tool technology over the Middle Stone Age (Mesolithic), as more and more archaeologists/prehistorians suggest, it is the domestication of plants and animals that is the **key** to other cultural changes in the Neolithic. The domestication of plants and animals changed the very core of cultural life and did it relatively quickly.

That's why many call it the "Neolithic Revolution." But because independent domestications occurred in various environments with different wild plants and animals to domesticate and under different cultural conditions, the other potential criteria to define the Neolithic are not universal. New tool types, pottery, evidence of settled rather than mobile existence, and villages are often found, but it is the domestication of plants and animals that generated those changes over previous hunter–gatherer and even **cultivation** times. (Cultivation is, by definition, taking care of *wild* plants and/or animals by guarding them, watering, and in the case of plants even moving them from their original location; but no genetic change occurs.) In a few Mesolithic locations, pottery was invented and used, and some settled habitation was required when people started cultivating previous to domestication. So some of the potential criteria occurred before the Neolithic. Since pottery, sedentism, new tools, and village life are not universal and sometimes occur in earlier cultural periods, they cannot be used to define the Neolithic.

But why is the term Neolithic only used in the Old World? Didn't Native Americans also independently invent agriculture? Why do archaeologists refer to domestication of plants and animals in the New World as NeoIndian? Definitions often change, but names of cultural periods seem to have a stable life of their own. In the Old World, cultural periods are referred to as the Paleolithic, Mesolithic, Neolithic, and Urbanism. In the New World, comparable cultural periods are referred to as the PaleoIndian, MesoIndian, NeoIndian, and UrbanIndian periods. Although both "worlds" had independent domestication events, there are important differences; perhaps the most important one being that New World domestication did not "take over" the lives of the people who invented or borrowed it, but was merely a small-scale add-on to their hunter–gatherer life styles.

We will therefore restrict our definition to the Old World and suggest the best definition of the Neolithic is that it is a cultural period in the Old World where domestication of plants and/or animals occurred. There are 5 areas in the Old World where archaeologists are confident there were independent inventions of domestication, and in all cases, plants were domesticated and, in most cases, animals as well. Let's see how each independent domestication, along with plants and animals, fits the definition. Beginning about 12,000 years ago, in chronological order they are: (1) the Near East with cereals such as wheat, barley, oats, and rye, and seeds such as peas and lentils along with sheep, goats, cattle, and pigs; (2) North China with millets along with pigs; (3) South China with dry rice along with chickens and water buffaloes; (4) Sub-Saharan Africa with millets, yams, sorghum, and African rice along with cattle and goats; and (5) New Guinea with bananas. In addition to cereals and seeds, different kinds of bulbs, roots, stems, fruits, and nuts were added to the lists in different areas, depending on the local wild plants.

Once archaeologists agree that the Neolithic should be defined as a cultural period in the Old World where domestication of plants and/or animals quickly took over, they can ask important questions about all 8 areas where domestication occurred (the other 3 are in the New World, one each in North, Central, and South America), such as: Why was the Neolithic such a "revolution" in the Old but not the New World? Why did people give up the easy life to take on the drudgery of farming? Why did villages and then towns develop when they are notoriously unhealthy, noisy, unfriendly, and dangerous? Why were people far less healthy under Neolithic conditions, living shorter lives than in previous time periods? Until archaeologists agree on definitions and specific criteria, they cannot look for the evidence that will answer these questions.

SPECIFYING "RACE"

The concept and definition of the term "race" has had a 180-degree turnaround during the last 30 years. Biological anthropologists have gone from defining "races" as groups of humans that differ biologically from other such "races" to claiming they do not exist, at least not in the biological sense. The biological concept of "race" has literally gone out of existence and that's why it is usually enclosed in quotation marks.

Let's look at some definitions of biological "races" made by well-known anthropologists and biologists before 1982:

- Theodosius Dobzhansky in 1944 said they were populations that differed in the incidence of certain genes.
- William Boyd in 1950 claimed they were populations that differed from other populations in the frequency of one or more genes.
- Stanley Garn in 1960 claimed they were breeding populations that were isolated from all others.
- Frederick Hulse in 1963 claimed they were groups that could be distinguished from one another on genetic grounds.
- Alice Brues in 1977 claimed they were groups that differed from others in the frequency of certain hereditary traits of external appearance who lived in particular geographic areas.
- Ernst Mayr in 1982 claimed they were aggregates that inhabited a geographic area and were a subdivision of a species.

A 1980 definition that puts these ideas together might define "race" as having 2 criteria: morphological and genetic differences from other such "races," and geographic isolation.

Thirty years later, biological anthropologists claim there are no such things as "races." Why? Because neither of the criteria that make up that circa 1980 definition is supported by evidence. The 2 criteria are (1) morphological/genetic distinctiveness and (2) geographic distinctiveness.

Ernst Mayr, probably the most well-known biologist of the twentieth century, used the term "subspecies" in his definition, suggesting he was as interested in the existence of subspecies in any animal group as he was in humans. So, let's start looking at the 2 criteria by way of asking if any animal species, human or not, has subspecies/races. Do dogs form subspecies? The answer is partially Yes to the first criterion and No to the second. Dogs that have "pedigrees" have been artificially selected by humans for hundreds of years and do show morphological/genetic similarities within their breeds (subspecies) and are different from other breeds. Breeds vary by size, color, shape, and temperament along with other traits: Irish setters are always large bodied, have long, red hair, long muzzles, and "good" temperaments. By contrast, bulldogs are always medium sized, have short hair, pug noses, and are "bad" tempered. In other words within each group, traits co-vary and are distinctive; this meets the first criteria of subspecies. But we all know there are a lot of dogs out there that are not pedigreed, but are "mongrels" of all sizes, colors, hair lengths, and temperaments. They would not fit the first criterion. Do dogs meet the second criterion of geographic distinctiveness/isolation? No, because people take their dogs with them when they move or see ads in a dog magazine and order a special dog from China or Africa.

Do baboons form subspecies? Yes and Yes relative to the 2 criteria. First, they are morphologically distinct, with each of the 5 subspecies having morphological/ genetic distinctiveness. The East African hamadryas baboon is large, with long light grey hair that is particularly long on the shoulders and heads of males, and with a long, pink muzzle. To the south, the anubis baboon is medium in size, with olive coloration, a shorter muzzle, and a black face. Even further south, the yellow baboon is medium in size, with yellow hair and a long, flat muzzle. In South Africa, the chacma baboon is medium in size, dark grey to black in color, and has a turned-up white-haired muzzle, while in West Africa the Guinea baboon is small and has "fluffy" reddish brown hair, with a flat muzzle. Some of these subspecies do hybridize on their borders for a short geographic space, but it does not seem to affect the majority of each group. Therefore, they are considered geographically distinctive as well as showing morphological co-variation.

And now for the real question, why don't humans meet the 2 criteria? First, and easiest, is the possibility that we form isolated or at least "distinctive" geographic groups. DNA analyses of both modern and fossil humans suggest that humans have been interbreeding showing gene flow "signatures," and migrating for hundreds of thousands of years. During 99.9 percent of our human history, our ancestors lived in small bands of 25 to 50 people where individual mating choices were very small. Assuming incest regulations were in place as well, it is also likely that males stayed in their home bands and females dispersed to neighboring bands, taking their genes with them to spread into the new population. What is called "stepping stone" breeding on borders means there were probably never any truly geographically isolated groups—at least not for long. And today, with over 6 billion of us humans traipsing all over the world, there is no such thing as an isolated population, and we are exchanging genes at a constantly accelerated rate.

The evidence that humans do not form morphologically/genetically distinctive groups today can be seen by looking at morphological traits. Just using similar traits used for baboons to conclude that they do form co-varying groups, let's look at the distribution of human skin color, stature, and head shape around the world and ask if those traits co-vary within groups. Do we find a "race" that always shows dark skin, tall stature, and broad heads, and another "race" that always shows light skin, short stature, and medium heads, and another "race" that always shows medium skin color, medium stature, and long/narrow skulls? The answer is No. Each of those 3 traits and its 3 variations varies independently of the others. (We know something about why there are these variations and why they vary independently, but that's another story.) We find all 9 combinations in populations around the world as well as "mongrels." Therefore, humans do not meet either criteria to have "races:" they are neither geographically nor morphologically distinctive. Biological anthropologists in the year 2010 agree that there are no such things as "biological races." That people perceive such things as "races" is based on ethnicity which is cultural, not biological. (See Chapter 11 for a further discussion of "race.")

The difficult and delicate issue of "races" among human beings has thus been clarified by the careful application of explicit criteria to human populations. In this case, we find that human populations do not reflect the criteria necessary to identify "biological races."

SPECIFYING FREEDOM

"Freedom" is an important general idea in Western and other cultures, both historically and currently. Philosophers have devoted much discussion to the meaning and nature of freedom and liberty, just as political leaders and citizens have devoted their actions and sometimes their lives to the pursuit of their visions of freedom. Anthropologists and social scientists who wish to explore freedom and liberty in their research must, as a first step, consider different and alternative meanings and establish a clear definition to guide them in their research.

In my (Salzman) current research project, which addresses the theoretical issue of the compatibility of freedom and equality, I have decided to follow John Stuart Mill's definition of freedom, which is that individuals can act, for good or ill, without the coercive interference of others. Having established the definition of freedom for the purposes of my research, I must next develop criteria to guide me in deciding whether or not particular individuals in the places that I am including in my research project are free to act without the coercive interference of others.

Before I go on with the criteria I developed for specifying "freedom," I would like to insert a reminder that the primary job of the anthropologist and social scientist is to study some part of the world as it is in actual reality and report on its nature. This used to be called "empirical" research and has been more recently referred to as "referential." Anthropological research is distinct from the analytic speculation and speculative analysis of the political philosopher, and from the ethical precepts and normative judgments of the moral philosophers and ethicists. While philosophers, politicians, and citizens generally may focus on the normative, on what should be, anthropologists and social scientists focus on the descriptive, on what really is, in the human and cultural worlds that they study. Therefore, for anthropologists, criteria for observing freedom in the cultures being studied allow us to say, yes, there is freedom or a certain degree of freedom in this, but not in that, in this particular place and time. Then, for theoretical purposes, the established description of freedom can be related to other factors, or "variables," in order to establish and explain relations between different factors, such as, in the case of my research, freedom, equality, and civil peace.

What criteria, then, am I using to study freedom? First, I have identified 10 areas of activity to examine an individual's freedom of action without interference:

- affiliation and association;
- childrearing and education;
- marriage;
- mobility and travel;
- occupation;
- ownership and property;
- political affiliation and opinion;
- religion and thought;
- residence; and
- speech.

For example, we can ask whether individuals can marry or not marry as they choose, and whether they are free to choose their partners. Or, do they lack freedom in that they must marry (or, alternatively, not marry) whether they like it or not; and, are their partners chosen for them by others (that is, an arranged marriage) rather than by themselves. Similarly, we can ask whether individuals are free to live wherever they like, or is residence restricted by kinship ties, community religion, or ethnicity, or by government regulation? Thus, I want to establish whether, and in what ways, individuals are free or restricted in 10 spheres of life.

At the same time, in regard to any sphere of activity, we need to judge the degree of freedom, or the severity of restriction. To do this, I will look at the negative sanctions, or punishments, imposed for a particular activity or behavior, on a continuum from no negative sanctions to the extremely strong negative sanctions:

- no negative sanctions;
- loss of good public opinion;
- loss of honor;
- loss of social or economic support;
- corporal punishment;
- incarceration;
- expulsion from group; and
- execution.

So, for example, if in a particular community individuals marry by their own choice but lose as a consequence their personal honor and the social and economic support of their community, we would have to judge freedom to marry considerably restricted. If we were to assign numerical values to sanction, say 0 for no sanctions, 2 for loss of public opinion, 4 for loss of honor, 5 for loss of social and economic support, 6 for corporal punishment, 8 for incarceration, 9 for expulsion, and 10 for execution, and we were to assign a number for the degree of freedom each of the 10 categories of activity (association, marriage, residences, and so on.), we would have a semi-quantitative index for that particular community or society. While such an index would be to a degree arbitrary, impressionistic, and simplistic, it is more systematic and precise than the way we usually discuss freedom, and it might prove to be a useful way of comparing one community or society with another.

CONCLUSION

With every general idea and concept that we use in anthropological research, we need, first, a clear definition so that we know, and can communicate, what we mean by that idea. Second, in order to pursue our research, we must specify a set of criteria to assist us in determining whether a specific person or population, activity, condition, or circumstance is or is not (or to what degree) an example of that idea or concept. Once you begin doing this regularly, you will be thinking anthropologically.

NOTE

1. This collaboration effort takes advantage of the fact that Salzman is a cultural anthropologist (writing here about nomadism and freedom) and Rice is a paleoanthropologist (writing here about the Neolithic and "race").

STUDY QUESTIONS

1. The first paragraph suggests we use general ideas in ordinary conversation that we should define before hand. Choose either "intelligence" or "democracy" and write your best definition, using criteria for possible research.
2. The concept of "subspecies" can be used for baboons, only halfway with dogs, and not at all with humans. Using the principles established, decide if cats can be thought of as having subspecies, defending your position.

CHAPTER 11

Thinking Anthropologically About "Race"

HUMAN VARIATION, CULTURAL CONSTRUCTION, AND DISPELLING MYTHS

Yolanda T. Moses

University of California Riverside

INTRODUCTION

Anthropologists have been studying the concept of "race" since the beginning of the field back in the eighteenth century. In the nineteenth century, there began a focus on evolutionary theory and looking for origins. In the twentieth century, the focus changed to debunking racial heritability theory (that is, biology) and promoting population genetics, clines, and genetics. And in the twenty-first century, anthropologists continue to look at the issue of "race," but with a more holistic approach. Research within the last 10 years centers on linking findings among geneticists, biological anthropologists, cultural anthropologists, archaeologists, and linguists. While I could have written a whole article or book on the contributions of each of these subfields of anthropology to theories about "race," neither time nor space permits this.[1]

Instead, this chapter will focus on linking 2 of the 4 fields of anthropology—human variation and culture—to explain the biocultural relationship of "race." A biocultural understanding of "race" will give you a more nuanced understanding of what anthropologists mean when they say there is no such thing as a "biological race." What we mean is that the concept of "race" within anthropology has changed over the years so that by the middle of the twentieth century, most anthropologists had dismissed the biological argument for "race" that existed in the nineteenth century. While saying that there is no such thing as a "biological race" may be confusing to you, one of the main points that I want to explore is that the idea of "race" continues to be a very powerful idea and does exist as a social and cultural construct. And, you should understand that one of the major outcomes of this cultural construction results in social inequality for many people in the United States, and that inequality continues today in an institutionalized form. That is, the presence of racial discrimination is not solely dependent on how individuals behave toward one another (**personal racism**) but is sustained by laws, policies, and practices separate from individual intent. This is called **institutionalized racism**. For a fuller explanation of personal versus institutionalized racism, see Kottak 2008; Mukhopadhyay, Henze, and Moses 2007; Mukhopadhyay and Henze 2003; Mukhopadhyay and Moses 1997.

MYTHS ABOUT RACE

Anthropologists know that just because we say there is no such thing as a "biological race," it does not mean that our words transform the way the general public views the issue. Based on over 20 years of university teaching and countless conversations with colleagues, I conclude that many students still believe that "biological race" is real. It is real in their worlds and constantly reinforced in popular culture by subtle and not so subtle newspaper articles that constantly refer to different groups of people as "racial" groups: for example, the recent announcement of the first drug for blacks (BiDil), and medical news that tells us certain groups are more prone to certain diseases than others (African Americans and hypertension, and Native Americans and hypertension, diabetes, and tuberculosis).

Based on interactions with students over the years, I believe that there are 3 widely held beliefs about "race" in American society:

1. Humans can be divided into at least 5 biologically distinct "races" (Caucasians, Africans, Asians-Pacific Islanders, Native Americans, and Australian Aborigines) because of the visible markers that these distinct groups display such as skin color, nose shape, and hair texture.
2. Athletic ability and "race" are linked, meaning that certain "racial" groups are better at certain sports than others—"it's in their genes."
3. "Race" and intellectual ability are linked based on the fact that certain "racial" groups consistently score higher on aptitude tests, such as the S.A.T. (Euro-Americans and Asian Americans) than other groups (African Americans and Hispanics).

Each of these myths will be addressed later, so you can evaluate each based on evidence presented in this chapter. I will be up front and tell you that I hope to convince you that there is overwhelming evidence that each is indeed a myth.

THE SCIENCE OF "RACE": THEN AND NOW

Then: Scientific "Race" in the Eighteenth and Nineteenth Centuries

How did anthropologists and their precursors demonstrate biological differences among groups before modern times?

The subject of evolution and evolutionary thought is controversial in some quarters—even today. Evolutionary theory originated in Western Europe, but many of its ideas were borrowed from people in other cultures including the Arabs, Indians, and Chinese.

Jean Baptiste Lamarck (1744–1829) was the first European scientist to attempt to explain the evolutionary process. He did so by describing the interaction between biological organisms and their environment. He believed that organic forms could be altered based on the increased or decreased use of their body parts. This came to be known as the use–disuse theory. The classic example is the giraffe's long neck: long necks evolved because giraffes needed them to eat leaves in the topmost branches of trees. Over time, giraffes with long necks survived and those with short necks did not and the trait of longer necks was passed on to offspring (this is the theory of acquired characteristics.) These early ideas about the evolutionary process were eventually discredited.

Thomas Malthus (1766–1834) was an English economist and clergyman whose writings about population increases inspired Charles Darwin and Alfred Russel Wallace to apply his ideas about human populations and food distributions to larger issues relative to the process of evolution. Malthus warned that we needed to pay attention to the fact that population size increases exponentially while food supplies remain pretty stable. This means that if left unchecked, human populations would outgrow their food supply. Darwin and Wallace used Malthus's ideas in the mid-1800s as the cornerstone of their theory of natural selection. How did this come about?

By the late 1830s, Darwin recognized that biological variation within a species was critically important for the survival of any species. In his paradigm-shifting book, *On the Origin of Species* (1859), Darwin saw, understood, and explained how selection in nature worked. It goes like this: in the struggle for existence, those individuals with favorable variations survive and reproduce; those with unfavorable variations do not. This way of thinking was controversial in its day because it did not attribute everything that happened in nature to God. The Christian Bible was thought to contain the most viable explanation for creation. Darwin's process of evolution also did not give any support to the notion of "progress."

Darwin's theory of natural selection gave rise to a nineteenth-century anthropological tradition focused on the classification and comparison of human populations and the search for indicators of mental and social capacity. This ushered in a focus on subspecies or "biological races." E. B. Tyler and Lewis Henry Morgan were cultural anthropologists who used the theory of natural selection to construct a "unilinear evolutionary theory" that ranked human groups along a continuum from the least civilized (savages) to the most civilized (European society). Physical indicators of evolutionary rank were developed, including skin color and the degree of facial projection (Blakey 1987; Smedley 2007). Measuring the size and weight of skulls/brains were 2 popular "scientific" ways to assess mental capacity and overall evolutionary ranking for "races," sexes, and immigrant groups to link their places in the evolutionary chain with their places in society, that is, linking biology with culture. Well into the twentieth century, anthropologists unfortunately were still engaged in devising psychometric and intelligence tests to support ideologies of so-called natural racial inferiority and superiority (Gould 1981).

Early in the twentieth century, Franz Boas, the father of American anthropology, began to challenge the dominant American racial ideology of the time that indicated that "People of Color" (African Americans, Native Americans, Chinese) and recent Eastern and Southern European immigrants were inferior to white Anglo-Saxon Protestants. By 1918, Boas had written over 50 publications on racial and biological topics alone. One of his most significant challenges to the biological racial determinists was his 1912 publication that challenged the dominant view that different "races" could be distinguished by obvious physical characteristics. Instead, he showed that in just one generation new immigrants could change their height, weight, head shape, and many other traits as a result of environmental factors such as better nutrition, clothing practices, and better general health (Smedley 2007).

The rise of population genetics from the 1930s to the 1950s provided additional evidence that challenged the dominant American worldview that there were distinct discernable "races," and that Euro-Americans were at the top of that hierarchy evolutionarily as well as socially and mentally. One summary suggests that "research focused on how basic evolutionary forces (genetic drift, migration, mutation, and natural selection) affected simple inherited traits such as the blood groups and hemoglobin polymorphisms rather than complex morphological and metric traits such as head shape or mental capacity" (Mukhopadhyay and Moses 1997:519).

Anthropologists who studied "race" were clearly undergoing a paradigmatic change in how "race" was conceptualized and measured in the biological world. During the 1950s, genetic systems were identified and mapped that showed conclusively that human traits are distributed in a non-concordant way; that is, humans display continuing variability in the distribution of many traits within and across environments. This came to be called clinal distribution (Livingstone 1964; Brace 1982). Another major nail in the coffin of "biological race" determinists was a demonstration that there is more variation within than between the so-called major "racial" groups (Lewontin 1972). This finding was subsequently reinforced with the discovery and use of more sophisticated DNA-based evidence.

Now

The late twentieth century saw additional breakthroughs in our understanding of human evolution and variation at the DNA level.

Several lines of molecular evidence have recently supported the "Out of Africa hypothesis" that claims a single place of human origin in Africa (Long

2004; Kidd, Rajeevan, and Osier et al. 2003). Many experts claim fossil and cultural diffusion evidence also support the idea that wherever our ancestors settled when they left Africa (perhaps 100,000 years ago), traveling to the Middle East, Asia, and eventually to Europe, Australia, and the Americas, those human groups interacted with their differing environments and developed both distinctive biological and cultural traits (Mukhopadhyay, Henze, and Moses 2007; Kottak 2008). Thousands of years later (during the age of colonization from the thirteenth through the twentieth centuries), some groups of people began to shift around the world again. Through immigration, both forced and elective, and through local and global migration, humans have been in continuous contact with each other biologically and culturally, exchanging both genes and ideas.

We humans have experienced the creation and amalgamation of new socially and culturally constructed groups for millennia. For an example close to home, the idea of the United States as a "melting pot" where successive waves of immigrants have been accepted and welcomed with open arms has always been a part of our folk belief system. In reality, it is a myth. The history of the United States is the cultural history of a country that has struggled with the paradox of promoting itself as the ideal of a color-blind pluralistic democracy on the one hand, while the reality is that it is a racially stratified society based on skin color, religion, and class. That has been a part of U.S. history since the inception of this country (Mukhopadhyay, Henze, and Moses 2007; Smedley 2007; Harrison 1995; Mullings and Marable 2000).

THE CULTURE OF "RACE": HOW DOES "RACE" GET SOCIALLY CONSTRUCTED?

Now that the idea of "biological race" has been shown to be incorrect, let's explore "race" as a social construction through the comparison of social stratification in 2 societies during the slavery period: the eastern Caribbean island of Montserrat and the southern United States.

The Caribbean Case for "Race": Montserrat

Both the idea and the realities of "race" in the eastern Caribbean developed along a different trajectory from the United States. I did fieldwork on the island of Montserrat in the eastern Caribbean in the early 1970s. Montserrat has been a British colony since the 1600s, but its recent claim to fame in the late twentieth century was the eruption of an ancient volcano forcing half of the population of 24,000 to be evacuated from the island. Because of its rough, mountainous terrain, the island never had large plantations like Jamaica, Barbados, or the southern colonies of Virginia, Georgia, or Mississippi. (Incidentally, most British people in the seventeenth century thought of the Irish, some of whom were imprisoned on the island, as a separate "race" of people only fit to be colonized by the British Crown.)

As a consequence of its small size and use as a penal colony, there were fewer black African slaves brought to Montserrat than to other plantation islands. Those who did come often worked side by side with the plantation owners on their small plantations of sugar cane and cotton. Almost as soon as slavery was abolished on Montserrat in 1838, the white British planters began to leave the island. Montserrat had a highly class and color based system during the period when slavery was legal just like the other islands, but mulattos or "mixed race" people were accorded a recognized place in this highly stratified social hierarchy. "Mixed race" people were allowed to buy their freedom, buy land, and accumulate wealth.

When slavery was abolished, mulattos and Europeans continued to live on the island and prosper. In this society, both color and class played a role in determining who "made it." Varying shades of color played a role, but social class could place a mulatto within the class structure even under the system of slavery. Many blacks left the island after slavery was abolished, but most of those who stayed became laborers or subsistence farmers and were still on the bottom of the stratification hierarchy (Moses 1976).

During the nineteenth and early twentieth centuries, the color/class hierarchy was relatively fluid on the island. Although there were no people of Middle Eastern descent there during the slavery period, they came later to Montserrat and other islands as merchants and store owners. They were accepted as a part of the middle class hierarchy. If a person (black, mulatto, European, or other white ethnicity) could educate himself or herself, own land or a business, he or she was considered middle class or even part of the elite island class hierarchy. By the mid-twentieth century, due to economic problems, many blacks, some mulattos, and a few whites began to migrate to other islands, to Latin American countries, and to northern countries in search of work. By the time I arrived on Montserrat to do my fieldwork in 1972, it had become a "sending" society, one that must export its workforce because there are not enough jobs or economic opportunities on the island (Moses 1976; Philpott 1973; Pulsipher and Pulsipher 2005).

The U.S. Experience

The Montserratian experience was unlike that of the United States after Emancipation in many ways. For example, the United States still had discrimination laws that prevented the newly freed slaves, Native Americans, and Chinese from becoming American citizens well into the twentieth century. Even immigrants from Ireland and eastern and southern Europe during the late nineteenth and early twentieth centuries had to jump over many hurdles to prove themselves "worthy" of being American citizens (Mukhopadhyay, Henze, and Moses 2007).

There are 2 major differences between the U.S. and the Montserratian experience of slavery and the social–racial stratification system that came out of it. The first is that while early colonial America did initially recognize mulattos as a separate category, the U.S. colonial government eventually hardened its laws in the colonies when slavery became more lucrative and only recognized the black–white dichotomy of "race." The law of "hypo-descent" or the "one drop rule" characterized whether a person was considered black or not. This had tremendous implication for inheritance of land and property, and who was considered free or not free in slave states. This law basically said that regardless of who your mother (often an African or "mixed race" slave) or father (often a white planter) were, if you had one drop of African blood, you were considered African, and therefore still a slave (Kottak 2008; Mukhopadhyay, Henze, and Moses 2007).

The second major difference was that there was no place in U.S. slave society for mulattos, or people of mixed ethnic or "racial" heritage. Even when some freed slaves (black and mulatto) did get an education and became economically middle class, there was no formally recognized status for them in North American society. They were often not able to buy land, or own a business or even a home. (This was true in the North as well as in the South.) Laws were passed at the local, state, and federal levels to keep African Americans from becoming viable social and economic participants in a growing American society (Smedley 2007). African Americans as a racial ethnic group in the United States have a history of freedom and emancipation closely tied to political fights to get discriminatory laws changed to free them from slavery (Thirteenth Amendment of the Constitution), to make them citizens of the United States (the Fourteenth Amendment), and to give them the right to vote (the Fifteenth Amendment). (The Fifteenth Amendment gave African American men, not women, the right to vote.) It was not until the Nineteenth Amendment was passed in 1920 that women in the United States finally got the right to vote. Because of discriminatory Jim Crow laws, most African Americans, male or female, were not able to vote in many Southern states until the passage of the voting rights laws of the Civil Rights Act passed in 1965. These laws were the direct result of the Civil Rights Movement. Affirmative Action policies that became law in 1965 intended to further level the playing field for African Americans. Those policies remain in effect today and are still being contested by conservative Americans who believe that it is unfair to give certain groups special treatment. In summary, the United States developed a legal system that defined black and white in narrow terms and ignored "mixed race" people and passed laws to systematically exclude them from participating as full citizens. This is the legacy of slavery, "race," and stratification in the United States. In Montserrat and other islands of the eastern Caribbean, the intersections of color, "race," and class allowed for more movement of people of African and of "mixed race" descent along their society's stratification continuum. (See Kottak 2008 for another example of the color, class, and "race" hierarchy, but in Brazil.)

STUDYING THE REALITIES OF "RACE": AN INTEGRATIVE BIOCULTURAL APPROACH

Several years ago, a number of anthropologists called for a more integrative biocultural approach to explain the complexities of "race" (Goodman and Armelegos 1996; Goodman and Leatherman 2001; Mukhopadhyay and Moses 1997; Mukhopadhyay and Henze 2003). This may sound a bit contradictory, but most anthropologists advocated decoupling "race" from biology under the old paradigm of the nineteenth- and early twentieth-century theories based on unilinear evolutionary theory, anthropometry, linking of physical and mental traits, measuring skin color, psychometric and intelligence testing, and making causal links among mental capacity, sociopolitical dominance, and inherited phenotypic traits. These ideas espoused by those early anthropologists and others helped to establish an elaborate set of hypotheses that unfortunately reinforced a pernicious biological and racial determinism that had far-reaching national and global implications. This was the old racial worldview that provided a rationale for slavery, colonialism and neocolonial domination, racial segregation, discrimination, and miscegenation laws, and fueled the **eugenics** movement in the United States and abroad as well as the anti-immigration movements in the United States in the nineteenth and twentieth centuries (Mukhopadhyay and Moses 1997).

But under the new integrative approach, we argue that we must *realign* the cultural and the biological, but within a radically different paradigm. This paradigm would situate human variation *within* a sociocultural framework, in effect reuniting culture and biology by imbedding biology in society and culture (Mukhopadhyay and Moses 1997). It is a tall order but we as cultural and biological anthropologists must rise to the challenge. We must be able to apply what we know about biological and cultural "race" to issues and problems of our contemporary society and world. We must be able to answer the question that students ask, "if races do not exist, then how do you explain the obvious differences that we see between and among ourselves?" The answer is what we see is not "race"; it is of course, human variation. And we need a biocultural approach to learn about *how* "race" is social constructed. We ultimately must be able to answer the question: through what processes have the American socially constructed racial categories become phenotypically marked and culturally real in our world? Understanding "race" in the United States requires understanding historical, sociocultural, and biological processes, and their interactions (Mukhopadhyay and Moses 1997).

How can you think anthropologically about "race" in an integrative biocultural way? One way is by looking at race through the lens of *human sexuality* and *reproduction*. We believe this is a fertile area of study for several reasons. The most obvious reason is that marriage, mating, and kinship data are the hallmarks of anthropology. We have been collecting these kinds of data from all over the world for over 100 years. By using this cross-cultural approach to look at social race and human variation, you can begin to think about some of the following interconnections and questions:

1. Human sexuality, marriage, and reproduction are culturally embedded and socially regulated phenomena that change over time in response to historical, ecological, cultural, political, economic, and demographic conditions. How are these cultural phenomena connected to normal distinct biological manifestations?

2. What are the human-devised strategies that regulate marriage, mating, and reproduction, including cross-cousin marriage, restrictions, homosexuality, celibacy (religious and voluntary), age, hypergamy, nineteenth-century

immigration restrictions that limited Chinese immigration to males, and American miscegenation laws that prohibited "interracial marriage"?

3. Societal strategies described above have had social, reproductive, and biological consequences. How have those strategies been essential to the creation and maintenance of American "races" socially and biologically over time? It is also important to look at how social group membership of women's offspring from culturally legitimate as well as non-sanctioned matings is assigned. (This is an area where both biological and cultural anthropologists can collaborate.)

4. How can biological and cultural anthropologists work together to amass data to include *why* there is no such thing as "biological race" by showing how social races are created and uncreated. For example, they can show the general disappearance of narrow ethnicities in the United States over time, such as, how did the Irish and Jews become "white folks" (Brodkin 1998) as they were assimilated and melted into the general "white population"? How did "Indo–Americans" lose their Caucasian status, and how did the merging (culturally and biologically) of Japanese Americans and Chinese Americans through intermarriage become classified by the U.S. census into a single generic group called Asian Americans?

In summary, a unified anthropological approach would examine both biological and cultural impacts and transformations. Anthropologists are uniquely equipped to take on this task because of the interdisciplinary nature of their work and the particular salience of a biocultural approach (Mukhopadhyay and Moses 1997).

"RACE": MYTH OR REALITY?

Let us now revisit the 3 myths suggested at the beginning of the chapter and hopefully convince you that they are not true:

Myth 1 tells us that humans can be divided into at least 5 biologically distinct named "races" because each group displays visible markers such as skin color, nose shape, and hair texture. This is false and therefore a myth because *Homo sapiens* is just one hugely variable species. As a species, we continue to be too mobile geographically and too intermixed biologically to have developed into separate species. The phenotypic differences that we observe such as skin color, nose shape, body shape, and hair texture are consequences of Darwinian selection into the variety of adaptive mechanisms that we humans have evolved to survive and thrive in different geographical environments. (See Jablonski and Chaplin 2005; Kottak 2008; Relethford 2007; and Mukhopadhyay, Henze, and Moses 2007.) There are no "biological races." Races are very real in a cultural sense, however, because our society and other societies around the world have culturally created them.

Myth 2 tells us that athletic ability and "race" are linked and that certain racial groups are better at certain sports than others. "It's in their genes." This is false because traits such as the ability to sprint, run long distances, dive, or drive a golf ball long distances are individual abilities, not group traits. That some Kenyans win long distance races is due to social, not biological selection. Social selection in Kenya and in other countries refers to the fact that sports, particularly those not requiring expensive equipment, became an outlet for members of certain groups in order to achieve elevated status. Both basketball and boxing provided a way out of the ghetto and for promoting ethnic pride for many American minorities during the first half of the twentieth century (Park 2003).

Myth 3 tells us that "race" and intellectual ability are linked based on the fact that certain "racial" groups consistently score higher on aptitude tests, such as the S.A.T. Go back to our conclusion to Myth 1, that these are not "biological races," just socially and culturally constructed groups. Old ideas about "biological races" are powerful and persistent, and issues of differences in IQ and intelligence get reinforced in racist pseudoscientific studies every few decades (A. Jenson 1969; R. J. Herrnstein and C. Murray 1994).

High scores on aptitude tests are mostly a function of socioeconomic status. That is, students tend to do better on these tests when they go to good schools, have money to pay for prep classes, and get reinforcement from their cultural environments. Individual aptitude or ability, not group aptitude or ability, is what is being measured here.

CONCLUSION

What anthropologists continue to learn about "race" is that it is a constantly shifting and changing complex and a complicated topic. It is highly charged politically as well. Anthropology's contribution to this topic involves the objective explanations of human variation and its history as well as new discoveries and what they do and do not mean at any given point in time. Anthropologists also provide a nuanced way to explain the concept of social race and its relationship to institutionalized as well as individual and personal racism. Finally, anthropology, because of its biocultural perspective, can hopefully help you think anthropologically about the concept of "race" both in your first classroom use of the concept and then later throughout your life.

NOTE

1. Archaeologists might point to ancient Egyptians' ideas about people around them, using "skin color" words to describe white people to the north, black people to the south, yellow people to the east, and themselves as brown. Biological anthropologists might point to the fact that the entire human species today is 99.9 percent alike in its genome.

REFERENCES

BLAKEY, M.
1987. "Skull Doctors: Intrinsic Social and Political Bias in the History of American Physical Anthropology—With Special Reference to the Work of Ales Hrdlicka." *Critique of Anthropology* 79(2): 7–35.

BOAS, F.

1912. *Changes in Bodily Form of Descendents of Immigrants.* New York: Columbia University Press.

BRACE, C. L.

1982. "Comment in Redefining Race: The Potential Demise of a Concept in Physical Anthropology." *Current Anthropology* 23: 48–49.

BRODKIN, K.

1998. *When Jews Became White Folks and What That Says about Race in America.* New Brunswick, NJ: Rutgers University Press.

GOODMAN, A. H. and G. J. ARMELEGOS

1996. "The Resurrection of Race: The Concept of Race in Physical Anthropology in the 1990s." In *Race and Other Misadventures: Essays in Honor of Ashley Montagu,* edited by L. T. Reynolds and L. Lieberman, pp. 174–186. Dix Hills, NY: General Hall Publishers.

GOODMAN, A. H. and T. LEATHERMAN

2001. *Building a New Biocultural Synthesis.* Ann Arbor, MI: University of Michigan Press.

GOULD, S. J.

1981. *The Mismeasure of Man.* New York: W.W. Norton & Company, Inc.

HARRISON, F.

1995. "The Persistent Power of 'Race' in the Cultural and Political Economy of Racism." *Annual Review of Anthropology* 24: 47–74.

HERRNSTEIN, R. J. and C. MURRAY

1994. *The Bell Curve: The Reshaping of American Life by Difference in Intelligence.* New York: Free Press.

JABLONSKI, N. G. and G. CHAPLIN

2005. "Skin Deep." In *Annual Editions, Physical Anthropology* (14th edition), edited by E. Angeloni, pp. 169–172. Dubuque, IA: McGraw-Hill/Dushkin.

JENSEN, A. R.

1969. "How Much Can We Boost I.Q. and Scholastic Achievement?" *Harvard Educational Review* 39(Winter): 1–123.

KIDD, K. H., RAJEEVAN, M. V., and OSIER, et al.

2003. "ALFRED—The Allele Frequency Data Base—An Update." *American Journal of Physical Anthropology* Supplement 36:128 (Abstract).

KOTTAK, C. P.

2008. *Cultural Anthropology* (12th edition). Boston, MA: McGraw-Hill.

LEWONTIN, R. C.

1972. "The Apportionment of Human Diversity." In *Evolutionary Biology,* edited by T. Dobzhansky et al., pp. 381–398. New York: Plenum.

LIVINGSTONE, F.

1964. "On the Nonexistence of Human Races." In *The Concept of Race,* edited by A. Montagu, pp. 46–60. New York: The Free Press.

LONG, J. C.

2004. "Human Genetic Variation: The Mechanisms and Results of Microevolution." Paper presented at the American Anthropological Association Annual Meeting, 2003. For an on-line version of this paper, see www.understandingrace.org.

MOSES, Y. T.

1976. *Female Status and Male Dominance in a West Indian Community.* Ph.D. dissertation. Riverside, CA: University of California.

MUKHOPADHYAY, C. C., HENZE, R., and Y. T. MOSES

2007. *How Real is Race: A Sourcebook on Race, Culture, and Biology.* Lanham, MD: Rowman and Littlefield Education.

MUKHOPADHYAY, C. C. and R. HENZE

2003. "How Real Is Race? Using Anthropology to Make Sense of Human Diversity." *Phi Delta Kappa* 84(9): 669–678.

MUKHOPADHYAY, C. C. and Y. T. MOSES

1997. "Re-establishing 'Race' in Anthropological Discourse." *American Anthropologist* 99(3): 517–533.

MULLINGS, L. and M. MARABLE (eds.)

2000. *Let Nobody Turn Us Around: An Anthology of African-American Social and Political Thought from Slavery to the Present.* Lanham, MD: Rowman and Littlefield.

PARK, M. A.

2003. *Introducing Anthropology: An Integrated Approach.* New York: McGraw-Hill.

PHILPOTT, S.

1973. *West Indian Migration: The Monserrat Case.* London, UK. London School of Economics Monographs on Social Anthropology.

PULSIPHER, L. M. and A. PULSIPHER

2005. *World Regional Geography: Global Patterns, Local Lives.* New York: Freeman Press.

RELETHFORD, J. H.

2007. *The Human Species. An Introduction to Biological Anthropology* (7th edition). Boston, MA: McGraw-Hill.

SMEDLEY, A.

2007. *Race in North America: Origin and Evolution of a World View.* Boulder, CO: Westview Press.

STUDY QUESTIONS

1. Write a paragraph about your personal opinion of each of the 3 "beliefs/myths" about "race".
2. Choose one of the 3 "myths," turn it into a question, and interview 3 people who are between 15 and 25, between 30 and 40, and over 50, asking that question. Write up your findings: are they the same or different for each group?

CHAPTER 12

Thinking with Gender

Paloma Gay y Blasco

University of St. Andrews

Anthropology is more than an academic discipline: it is a way of approaching the world and our place in it. Anthropology's starting point is the awareness of difference and variability between ways of thinking, ways of acting, and ways of being in the world of different groups of humans. You will know you are beginning to think anthropologically when, faced with how other people live, you start to interrogate your most deeply held assumptions about how things are. Thus, at the core of the anthropological approach is the capacity to use our knowledge about others, whether in the past or the present, and to question what we take most for granted. And some of our most deep-seated, most unquestioned assumptions have to do with what we believe men and women to be like, how we expect ourselves and others to act, think, and feel as men or women. For example, we "know" that men are more rational and women more emotional, that men bottle up their feelings, and women share their feelings with their friends. We expect women to want to take care of their children and men to want to be successful in their careers. Crucially, we also "know" that this is because of their different biology. We see men and women as physically and hence socially different, pushed by their bodies toward particular roles and inclinations.

The discipline's drive to question our assumptions about men and women can be traced back as far as the late nineteenth century, when "armchair anthropologists" like Lewis Henry Morgan and Jakob Bachofen imagined a distant past in which women, rather than men, ruled. And then in the early twentieth century, writers as diverse as Bronislaw Malinowski, Margaret Mead, and Phyllis Kaberry used detailed analyses of Papua New Guinea, Samoa, Africa, and Aboriginal Australia to show that relations between the genders display huge variability: that what we take to be the norm in the ways men and women behave is in fact just one among many possibilities.

For example, Margaret Mead described how, in 3 neighboring Papua New Guinea tribes, people had very different notions of masculinity and femininity. Whereas the Arapesh expected both men and women to have what we would describe as "warm and maternal temperaments" (Mead 1963:40), among the Mundugumor "both men and women are expected to be violent, competitive, aggressively sexed" (ibid.:225). Among the Tchambuli, by contrast, "the woman is the dominant, impersonal, managing partner, the man the less responsible and emotionally dependent person" (ibid.:279). What Mead found striking was that none of these groups had ideas that fitted those dominant in North America or Western Europe at the time she was writing. Although her approach and material have been criticized, her book *Sex and Temperament in Three Primitive Societies* was successful in that it demanded that anthropologists challenge their own preconceived notions when considering relations between the genders.

Almost 40 years later, in the early 1970s, some anthropologists took up this challenge in a new and wholly transformative direction.[1] Inspired by the rebirth of feminism and also by the spread of various forms of political radicalism, they scrutinized how anthropology had represented men and women throughout the twentieth century. As feminists and as scholars, they argued that Euro–American expectations had indeed molded anthropological depictions of past and present peoples as well as of hominids and nonhuman primates. Our discipline, they emphasized, carried heavy cultural baggage: because this was how things were expected to work back home, what appeared "natural" and appropriate for decades anthropologists had taken for granted—that men would be in charge and that they would be the ones running the affairs of the community, while women would raise the children, take care of the home, and tend to the elderly. Starting in the 70s and continuing in the 80s, **sociocultural anthropology**, biological anthropology, and archaeology alike were shown to be androcentric disciplines, where men and their perspectives were the focus of attention and where women were rendered invisible and their voices muted. Because women make up 50 percent of the population, by ignoring women, their activities and worldviews, anthropologists had put forward incomplete, skewed, and inaccurate accounts. Even more importantly, feminists argued, anthropologists' masculinist bias had not just restricted the kinds of topics they wrote about, but the very questions they asked and the theories and concepts they deployed in order to answer them.

Take, for example, an important distinction between the domestic and the public spheres, which was essential to economic and political anthropology and to archaeology throughout the twentieth century. Feminist scholars argued that this distinction was dependent on Western beliefs about men's and women's roles in biological reproduction, which were assumed to lead to a division of activity and space. In particular, the tie between mothers and children and the work that women do as mothers were seen as both natural and universal, and to have the same consequences for social organization everywhere. Instead, feminist anthropologists produced ethnographic evidence from both Western and non-Western societies to show that "mothering work" can be and is often done by people other than the mother—such as grandparents, nannies, fathers, or friends. And, even when women are in charge of what we would call domestic tasks, the separation between spheres may still be problematic. Eleanor Leacock (1980), in her account of the lives of Iroquois women before colonization, argued that "household management was itself the management of the public economy." Because women controlled the distribution of food, they could influence or even veto war declarations, religious festivals, councils, and hunting expeditions. What happened in "the domestic" was essential to "the public," and the two could not be conceptualized as distinct.

Another example of feminist revisionism concerns our understanding of human evolution. Until the 1970s, anthropology embraced the "Man the Hunter" model. This revolved around the notion that it was the activities of males, in particular their hunting of large dangerous mammals, that were the driving force in hominid evolution, leading to language acquisition, tool development, bipedalism, and larger brain size. Females, on the other hand, were portrayed as "peripheral to our evolutionary history" (Hager 1997:4): they were "responsible for producing and caring for their offspring—but not much else" (ibid.:1).

Then feminist anthropologists argued that the "Man the Hunter" depiction of human evolution was shaped by a broader masculinist, chauvinistic worldview that dominated Western society and hence also the sciences. Sally Slocum, Adrienne Zihlman, and Nancy Tanner put forward the "Woman the Gatherer" model, arguing that female hominids provided the lion's share of the diet through their gathering of plant foods and small-animal hunting; and they were also tool makers (Slocum 1975; Tanner and Zihlman 1976; Zihlman 1978). Females, it seemed, played as important a role in human evolution as males.

By questioning women's and men's "natural" roles, feminist anthropologists and archaeologists in fact challenged what their disciplines had taken to be the obvious, "natural" shape of human societies, separated into socially and culturally significant activities and arenas (male), and domestic, private, less significant domains (female). This meant scrutinizing the activities and worldviews of men and women, and their positions in society: Are men everywhere in charge of the decisions that affect all in the community? Are women always primarily concerned with reproduction? And, because in our Euro–American and anthropological framework the domestic and the public are not just separate but hierarchically ranked, anthropologists and archaeologists also had to ask crucial questions about the production of gender hierarchies and inequalities: Are women everywhere subordinated to men? Have men always been dominant? Why does gender inequality exist? How does it come about, and how is it sustained? In their responses, some authors looked for universal explanations for gender inequality, theories that would fit all situations. Others argued that, in different contexts, women experienced different kinds and degrees of subordination. So, it was necessary to identify the specific constellation of social, cultural, economic, and political factors that generate a distinct form of inequality in each particular milieu.

Feminist anthropologists and archaeologists soon realized that, in trying to respond to these fundamental issues, they were grappling with 2 central preoccupations common to all anthropology. The first of these has to do with the validity of our analytical tools: if anthropological theories and concepts are part and parcel of a broader, North, Euro–American cultural tradition, what kind of knowledge of others do we produce? Or, even more radically, if there are important elements within this tradition of which we tend to remain oblivious, can we ever be faithful to the experiences of the people we study? For example, how can we be sure that what to us looks like gender inequality or even outright oppression—think for example, female circumcision—is in fact conceptualized and experienced as such by those involved? The second preoccupation has to do with the fact that, in the West, we tend to explain the different positions of men and women in society by reference to their bodies. In our view, it is because men and women have different bodies that they do different things and have different roles and responsibilities. This means that it is difficult for anthropologists and archaeologists, as Westerners, to explain gender relations except *as a consequence* of physical sexual differences. But, is this all there is to gender everywhere? How are we to think about the relationship between the body and human social and cultural activity? By the 1980s, feminist anthropologists had moved way beyond Mead's emphasis on the cross-cultural variability of gender roles and stereotypes, and found themselves debating the reach, character, and purpose of anthropological knowledge itself.

THINKING ABOUT INEQUALITY

One area that has thrown into particular relief these questions of translation, interpretation, and knowledge is the study of gender inequality. And one anthropologist who has argued particularly successfully for the need to scrutinize closely the contents of our conceptual toolbox has been Marilyn Strathern. She carried out fieldwork in Mount Hagen in Papua New Guinea, where women work hard raising pigs and growing coffee as a cash crop. However, it is the men who take the bulk of the coffee proceeds, and they also use the pigs in ceremonial exchanges that also include money and shell valuables. Women are encouraged to contribute their small savings toward men's ventures—such as the buying of a truck—and are themselves exchanged for valuables when given in marriage to other clans. Here, we seem to be confronted with a clear case of gender inequality and female subordination. In as much as women hand over their money to men, rather than spending it themselves, and since they appear to be treated as "things" in marriage exchanges, from a Western perspective they are clearly being exploited. And yet, Strathern asks us to think harder: because Western and Melanesian notions of the person are so different, "we cannot simply extend Western feminist insights to the Melanesian case" (1988:7).

In the West, Strathern argues, we have a commodity economy and a commodity way of thinking that opposes persons to things: persons transact things, and for persons to be transacted means a diminution of their agency and hence of their personhood. Moreover, in Western commodity economies, rights over property reflect the activity of a person in generating that property. If somebody is not properly paid for their work, we consider their activity to have been overlooked: they have been exploited because their labor has not been purchased but stolen from them. That person then has been treated, not as an active subject, but as an object, somebody who does not control his or her labor or produce, in effect a slave. This is the perspective that a standard feminist analysis of gender relations in Mount Hagen would take, considering the extent to which Hagen women retain control over their labor and produce, and to which they themselves are objectified. And yet, Strathern tells us that the distinction between subject and object (that is so central to Western thinking about inequality and hence also to both feminism and anthropology) does not work for Mount Hagen. Rather than a commodity economy, Hagen thinking and social relations are best conceptualized through the model of the gift. Whereas commodities can be alienated from their producer or their owner, gifts cannot: in gift exchange, the objects exchanged create bonds between persons since, as Marcel Mauss says, "to give something is to give part of oneself" (1954:10). Since objects given in gift exchange always embody the person who gives them, the distinction between persons and objects does not help us understand relations between men and women in Mount Hagen. Women here are not treated as objects in the Western sense, nor are their pigs and coffee alienated from them.

This Melanesian example is relevant because it illustrates issues that lie at the core of feminist anthropology as both an intellectual and a political enterprise. On the one hand, if our concepts do not account for the way the people of Hagen think about men and women, how are we to explain gender inequality there? Can we talk about gender inequality at all in this particular situation? Or, should the term be reserved for those ethnographic contexts where our own concepts are more closely mirrored? On the other hand, whether or not the women of Mount Hagen use concepts similar to ours, is it still possible or desirable to argue that they are underprivileged by comparison with the men? Might it be that local concepts and worldviews hide from the women the truth of their situation? Could these concepts be instrumental in generating their disadvantage? These questions become even more significant and difficult when we remember that feminist anthropology has a feminist and not merely an anthropological agenda. If we can no longer make female subordination a straightforward matter, on what shall we base feminism as a movement for social transformation?

This problem became particularly urgent to feminist anthropologists in the mid-1980s, when black feminists, particularly in the United States, argued forcefully against the notion of "universal sisterhood" that had dominated feminism throughout the previous decade. Gender, these writers explained, cannot be considered in isolation from race (or class or ethnicity): "the woman who is seen as inferior because of her sex can also be seen as superior because of her race, even in relationship to men of another race" (Carby 1982:221). Black and white women, and black and white men, experience patriarchy very differently. This meant that feminism itself had to be redefined to take into account women's conflicting roles and positions, for example as oppressors and not just as victims. By the late 1990s, both archaeologists and anthropologists working on gender were focusing on how differences, hierarchies, and inequalities between *and* among men and women are produced and sustained. They were also producing a highly reflexive anthropology, premised on the recognition that, while we can never detach ourselves completely from our own way of conceptualizing the world, we should make visible its impact on our accounts and analyses (Strathern 1988).

THINKING ABOUT THE BODY

Throughout the 70s, 80s, and 90s, much fruitful debate emerged from anthropologists' growing awareness of the need to reexamine our analytical tools—to treat our own worldview anthropologically, putting it under the lens just like we do with the ideas of the people we study. More recently anthropologists have extended this reflexive standpoint to one key area, our ideas about the human body and, in particular, about sex. The notion that men and women have different roles, different inclinations, and different existential and emotional dispositions *because* they play different roles in reproduction is central to our Euro–American way of thinking about and being in the world. The binary sexed body appears incontestable as the source of our identities so that, in our everyday lives, we rarely question its explanatory primacy or even ask what that sexed body *is*. This is because of how we tend to think about the relationship between the natural/biological and the cultural worlds, and also because we live in a society where scientific and pseudoscientific information about the body is constantly being disseminated for example through the media. We usually consider this information to be reliable and true, unsullied by preconceptions or stereotypes, existing beyond the reach of culture.

And yet, feminist anthropologists and others, like historians of science, have shown that scientific knowledge of the body is very much the product of its time and place. It reflects the broader social and cultural conditions of its production, and it embodies the worldviews and beliefs of the scientists who produce it. In the case of knowledge of sexual difference, it tends to encapsulate and reproduce our ideas about what kinds of social persons men and women are and should be like. Take Emily Martin's work on scientists' accounts of the meeting between the egg and the sperm, the moment of conception, as a "scientific fairy tale" (2001). In scientific textbooks, Martin explains, the egg and the sperm behave respectively in stereotypically feminine and masculine ways. For example, the egg is portrayed as passive, it "does not move or journey, but passively 'is transported,'" is swept, "or even 'drifts'" (2001). By contrast, sperm are small, "streamlined," and invariably active. They "deliver" their genes to the egg, "activate the developmental program of the egg," and have a "velocity" that is often remarked upon. Their tails are "strong" and "efficiently powered" (ibid.).

Egg and sperm are endowed in these accounts with different kinds of gendered agency: the egg appears as a "damsel in distress," waiting to be fertilized or die; the sperm as "heroic warrior to the rescue" (2001). Martin explains how even newer, revisionist depictions of the moment of conception continue to draw on dominant gender stereotypes, this time describing the egg through the image of the dangerous woman, the "female aggressor who 'captures and tethers' the sperm . . . rather like a spider lying in wait in her web" (2001).

For feminist sociocultural anthropologists, the awareness that scientific knowledge of the body is contextual is important because of two key reasons. First, this awareness enables us to interrogate our taken-for-granted notion that social conventions about gender have a "natural" or "biological" basis—that we are the way we are simply because our bodies make us so. We can therefore start to investigate how these conventions come about, how they are reproduced, and whether they are, could be, or should be challenged. Second, we can investigate the ways knowledge of the body is produced, by scientists and by others, in the contemporary West and also in other geographic and past contexts. How do some accounts of the body become not just acceptable but normative? Which stories and which elements of the body are taken up and which are dropped by the side? And why? How do these stories relate to men's and women's positions in particular social and historical contexts?

This focus on the production of knowledge of the body has been central to my own work with Spanish Gitanos (Gypsies/Roma), in which I have researched their particular experience of the body and model of physiology, as well as the role this model plays in the Gitanos' relationship with a dominant non-Gitano society. In my case, it was the difficulties I had in taking Gitano descriptions of the female body at face value that led me to consider how to theorize knowledge of the body produced by "Others."

Soon after I started doing fieldwork in Madrid, I realized that Gitanos put an enormous value on the preservation of female virginity until marriage. The fact that Gitano women were chaste and that they had sex only with their husbands, I was told again and again, was what made the Gitanos different from, and better than, the non-Gitanos who marginalized and oppressed them. A girl could marry in two ways, the Gitanos explained to me: by having first-time sex with a boy, and then eloping with him to the house of a relative (this was the less prestigious option); or with a wedding ceremony in which she was ritually deflowered (the high-prestige route). So far, so good. But I soon became puzzled: this ritual defloration did not consist of the girl having sex with her fiancé, and there was no mention of breaking the hymen. Instead, the ceremony involved only women. While the men partied outside, married women and the bride would go to a room apart. There the girl would lie down, and open her legs. An experienced, older woman, a professional "deflowerer" or *ajuntaora* (literally a join-er) would wrap a clean handkerchief around her forefinger and push it into the girl's vagina. She would then "burst the grape," a little ball inside the vagina that contained the girl's honor, her *honra*. This was a yellow liquid and the aim of the procedure would be to produce some large stains (called "flowers") on the handkerchief, about 2 inches in diameter. Sometimes some blood would also come out, and this was considered a sign of the inexperience of the *ajuntaora*. The girl's mother-in-law would keep the handkerchief. Once the defloration was over, the girl and her fiancé would be paraded around on the shoulders of relatives amidst much celebration and merrymaking. The expectation of the defloration ceremony meant that girls were much concerned with protecting their virginity in their everyday lives, not wearing trousers that might "spoil their vaginas," not using tampons, and, of course, not having penetrative sex.

Throughout my fieldwork I kept wondering what the *honra* and the "grape" were. Did they really exist? I had examined carefully some defloration handkerchiefs, and been puzzled by the round, yellow stains. But for this physical evidence, I would have thought that it was all in the minds of the Gitanos. Then I learned about the Bartholin's Glands, which exist inside the vaginas of all women, which are roughly the size of a grape, and which discharge a lubricating fluid during intercourse. It seemed fairly likely that the Gitanos' "grape" and the Bartholin's Glands were the same thing. Yet, like the majority of Western women (and men), I had been unaware of their existence. Unlike the breasts, the vagina, or the XX chromosomes, these glands played no role in my own understanding of what makes a woman. I reached the conclusion that the Gitanos did not overlook the body when considering what men and women are like: on the opposite, the sexed body was essential to how they managed to resist assimilation into the aggressive non-Gypsy world. But their views of what this sexed body consisted of, and the way they experienced it, challenged my non-Gitano ideas of what makes a body female.

In archaeology, with its emphasis on material practices and traces, the processes through which the body comes to be known as male, female, both, or even neither, have been the focus of particular attention. In their analysis of Cypriot prehistoric figures, Bernard Knapp and Lynn Meskell (1997) argue that we cannot assume that our binary dichotomy, where male and female are seen as opposite and where bodies cannot be both male and female at the same time, necessarily applies to other contexts. They argue that these figurines, which have traditionally been explained by anthropologists as representations of mother goddesses, do not represent either males or females. Rather, the figurines evidence a concern with displaying the growing sense of self-identity that developed hand in hand with increasing social complexity during the Chalcolithic period. At least some of these figurines represent, "an attempt at harmonizing, or at least incorporating, the sexual characteristics of males and females" within one single body (ibid.:194). Other archaeologists have similarly focused on objects as evidence of the practices through which bodies acquire a normative or "socially acceptable" gender, shifting their analyses from "a system of classification and hierarchy grounded in the facts of biology" to looking for evidence of the "reproduction of a culturally specific way of gendering persons," which may not fit well with the 2-sex, 2-gender system that we tend to take for granted (Joyce 2006:51).

Biological anthropologists have also taken up the challenge, even though at first sight the notion that scientific knowledge of the body is contextual may seem particularly problematic for this discipline (Fedigan 1997). Indeed, it has not always been easy for biological and sociocultural anthropologists to communicate fruitfully regarding the feminist critique of science. Some biological anthropologists have been dismayed by the ease with which their sociocultural colleagues have reduced evidence to the status of "stories," while the latter have been accused of disregarding the materiality of the body and the limits that it imposes on what is possible in terms of human action. And yet, feminist biological anthropologists have successfully argued for the need to acknowledge that science is socially constructed while continuing to investigate the roles that biology plays in human behavior and evolution (Sperling 1991). They have reflected on how they themselves produce knowledge of sex in connection with both humans and primates, and they have analyzed the implications of this knowledge to develop our understanding of the past and of the present. A good example is Lori Hager's review of the sexing of the *Australopithecus afarensis* fossil "Lucy" as a female. She tells us that, not only was this sexing influenced by unexamined assumptions about maleness and femaleness in the part of the original researchers but also, crucially, "the 'femaleness' of this particular fossil became crucial" to later interpretations of other remains. Hager argues convincingly that "our view of females early in prehistory was essentially shaped the very day that 'Lucy' was found" (1997:21), and her analysis opens up the way for a reevaluation of the evidence and an improvement of our understanding of the past.

CONCLUSION

The contribution of feminist anthropology to the discipline has been immense and transformative. Over the last 40 years, we have learned not only to think anthropologically about gender but also to use gender to think about anthropology. As a consequence, we have reviewed our models and analytical tools; we have become aware of the stereotypes and taken-for-granted notions that influence our conclusions; and we have reevaluated the status of the knowledge that we produce. We have asked fundamental questions about power, inequality, and human motivation, and about the very nature and distinctiveness of humanity. Thinking with and about gender has indeed become essential to the way anthropology faces the contemporary world.

NOTE

1. Whereas the feminist critique of sociocultural anthropology took place in the 1970s, archaeologists had to wait until the early 1980s for a similar movement to reshape their discipline. It was in 1984 that Margaret Conkey and Janet Spector argued for the first time that archaeology had perpetuated a "gender mythology" by reproducing contemporary Western gender stereotypes.

REFERENCES

CARBY, H.
    1982. White Woman Listen! Black Feminism and the Boundaries of Sisterhood. In *The Empire Strikes Back: Race and Racism in 70s Britain*. London: Hutchison.
FEDIGAN, L. M.
    1997. "Is Primatology a Feminist Science?" In *Women in Human Evolution*, edited by L. D Hager. New York: Routledge.

HAGER, L. D.
1997. "Sex and Gender in Paleoanthropology." In *Women in Human Evolution,* edited by L. D. Hager. New York: Routledge.

JOYCE, R. A.
2006. "Feminist Theories of Embodiment and Anthropological Imagination: Making Bodies Matter." In *Feminist Anthropology: Past, Present and Future,* edited by P. L. Geller and M. K. Stocker. Philadelphia: University of Pennsylvania Press.

KNAPP, A. B., L. M. MESKELL.
1997. "Bodies of Evidence on Prehistoric Cyprus." *Cambridge Archaeological Journal* 7(2): 183–204.

LEACOCK, E.
1980. "Montangais Women and the Jesuit Program for Colonisation." In *Women and Colonisation: Anthropological Perspectives,* M. Etienne and E. Leacock, eds. New York: Praeger.

MARTIN, E.
2001. *The Woman in the Body: A Cultural Analysis of Reproduction.* Boston: Beacon Press.

MAUSS, M.
1954 (1925). *The Gift: Forms and Functions of Exchange in Archaic Societies.* London: Cohen and West.

MEAD, M.
1963. Sex and Temperament in Three Primitive Societies.

SLOCUM, S.
1975. "Woman the Gatherer: Male Bias in Anthropology." In *Toward an Anthropology of Women,* edited by R. Reiter. New York. Monthly Review Press.

SPERLING, S.
1991. "Baboons with Briefcases vs. Langurs in Lipstick: Feminism and Functionalism in Primate Studies." In *Gender at the Crossroads of Knowledge: Feminist Anthropology in the Postmodern Era,* edited by M. di Leonardo. Berkeley, CA. University of California Press.

STRATHERN, M.
1988. *The Gender of the Gift: Problems with Women and Problems with Society in Melanesia.* Berkeley: University of California Press.

TANNER, N. and A. ZIHLMAN.
1976. "Women in Evolution. Part I. Innovation and Selection in Human Origins." *Signs: Journal of Women in Culture and Society* 1(3): 585–608.

ZILHMAN, A. L.
1978. "Women in Evolution. Part II. Subsistence and Social Organization among Early Hominids." *Signs: Journal of Women in Culture and Society* 4(1): 4–20.

STUDY QUESTIONS

1. Before you read this chapter, you must have had some personal thoughts about how men and women differ in American culture. What were they?
2. What makes a body male? What makes a body female? Are these descriptions cultural or biological or both? How do we know?

CHAPTER 13

Fieldwork: Collecting Information

Philip Carl Salzman
McGill University

Barbara J. King
College of William and Mary

Norah Moloney
Institute of Archaeology, University College London

Norma Mendoza-Denton
University of Arizona

Most practicing anthropologists do fieldwork throughout their lives; a lot of them decided on anthropology as a career because they wanted to do fieldwork and realized that they could live with Iranian nomads, observe gorillas in Uganda, excavate a Neolithic village, or learn an exotic language in New Guinea and spend summers, sabbaticals, and funded research years in an international setting. For many, it is the highlight of their lives.

But because the different subfields of anthropology specialize in a particular aspect of what it is to be human, fieldwork differs from one subfield to another. While cultural anthropologists might focus on the culture of a non-Western society, biological anthropologists might want to find and analyze a new species of hominids in our ancestral lineage or observe primates in their modern habitats for clues to primate universals or differences, archaeologists might focus on the culture of our prehistoric (or historic) past through excavation of tools or other artifacts of past societies, and anthropological linguists might look for "lost" languages, or compare one language with another, or engage in analyzing the uses of language. Because of these specialties, it is rare to find any single anthropologist doing fieldwork in more than one subfield; occasionally a bioanthropologist is also an archaeologist, and occasionally a cultural anthropologist studies the language of the group he or she is studying as part of the greater cultural story.

Therefore, we asked 4 teaching anthropologists who consistently do fieldwork in a single subfield to write about their own fieldwork to give you a feeling for actually being in the field. There are both joys and sorrows in doing any kind of fieldwork from friendly or unfriendly "natives" and government officials to health risks. We continue to do it because the joys of discovery outweigh the sorrows. The essays below on fieldwork are in the order they were submitted: cultural anthropology, biological anthropology, archaeology, and linguistic anthropology. We hope you get the flavor of doing fieldwork in each subfield; each has a common theme in that it is studying what it is to be human.

Cultural Anthropology

Philip Carl Salzman
McGill University

"What happens when members of the tribe fight with one another?" I asked Shams A'din, who was to become my closest friend during my research. This was early in my ethnographic fieldwork among the Shah Nawazi nomadic tribe in southeastern Iran, a region called Baluchistan. "Oh," said Shams A'din, "we don't fight; we are all brothers."

I traveled to southeastern Iran to conduct research on ecology and politics among tribesmen making a living in a very arid, desert region. From my reading and thinking about human behavior and culture, and about politics and ecology, I had a general orientation, or understanding, that we could call "theory." I also had some specific ideas about how tribes work and the interrelations between ecology and politics, that we call "hypotheses." But I did not really have factual knowledge about what tribes in Baluchistan actually do. That is why I undertook field research to collect information about what tribesmen really do, and so to test my hypotheses and see if my theory had been helpful.

When I asked Shams A'din questions, I was using a research technique to collect information. I was interviewing him. His answers were information for me. But, and here it gets a little complicated, how was I to understand his answer? Was Shams A'din trying to please me by telling me what he thought I wanted to hear? Was he trying to mislead me, on the grounds that knowledge held by others is dangerous? Was he trying to describe behavioral reality in the world as it is? Or was he describing the tribe as he wished it were?

Information that we collect, as you see, is not always transparent, that is, clear as to what it means and how we should take it. If we take it one way or another, that is what we might call our interpretation. To do our job of collecting information well, we must realize that there are alternative interpretations, and so we must be cautious in our conclusions.

Cultural anthropology has a way of constructively addressing these complications. During our field research, we engage in what we call "participant observation." This dignified phrase means "hanging around with the folks and trying to figure out what they are up to." There are two main strategies in participant observation: one is long-term residence among the people you are trying to understand. The other is using a variety of information-gathering techniques to collect diverse kinds of information and also to check and cross-check information collected.

In addition to interviewing, asking people questions, another basic technique is watching what people do. It is not uncommon—we see it enough in our lives back home—that people say one thing and do another. So when your informants (i.e., people giving you information) tell you things, you should keep an eye out to see if what they do is consistent with what they tell you. If what they do is inconsistent with what they have told you, then further clarification is required. So when I saw conflicts and fights develop among tribesmen, I wondered about what Shams A'din had told me. "Shams A'din," I said, "you told me that fellow tribesmen were brothers and never fought, but here are the Dadolzai and the Kamil Hanzai fighting with one another." "We should not fight; we are *yeki*, one. But if a fight starts, we must support our closer kinsmen against more distant kinsmen." So Shams A'din's first answer to me was correct, as a description of ideal behavior, of correct normative behavior. But to understand it as a description of actual behavior, of what people really did, would have been a mistake.

So, the cross-checking of information from different information-gathering techniques can clarify the information from any one source and aid one in insuring a realistic understanding. In addition to interviewing and direct observation, there is a whole raft of techniques that cultural anthropologists use:

- Counting and measuring population, housing area, livestock, products, participation, conflicts, exchanges, marriages, children, etc.;
- Case studies of particular events as they develop and generate consequences;
- Tests: personality, cognition, intelligence, knowledge, memory, dexterity, strength, skill, stamina, etc.;
- Participation in, or direct experience of, local work tasks, artistic expression, ritual occasions, etc.

Within interviewing itself, there are a variety of techniques that, if used, could also serve for cross-checking:

- Informal, casual discussions;
- Formal interview at a designated time and place;
- Formal interview with open-ended questions, allowing the informant to reply as he or she likes;
- Formal interview with alternative answers specified;

- Formal interview eliciting networks of kinship, friendships, partnerships, and/or influence, to provide information for network analysis; and
- Formal interview eliciting autobiographical account in which the informant tells about her or his life.

Observation too can be carried out in different ways that complement one another and can serve as cross-checks:

- Casual observation of what one happens to see;
- Systematic observation of work techniques, gender relations, rituals, child-rearing, decision-making, relations with the environment, effects of climate, etc.;
- Opportunistic observation of conflicts, innovations, change, coercion, entrepreneurship, enforcement of norms, etc.

We anthropologists have many techniques in our information-gathering quiver. The more we use, the fuller and more complete our information will be. For this reason, when I do field research, I am sure to use them all. Okay, this is a huge lie. No anthropologist uses more than a few of these techniques in a year of fieldwork. Why not use more, if it would improve the information base? The reason is simple: each of these techniques is hugely time and energy consuming, and doing a few exhausts our time and energy resources. Here practical reality triumphs over ideal fieldwork practice. Anthropologists, like everyone else, are imperfect, and we do the best we can with the limited resources available.

Furthermore, we are often held up in our research by limitations of language capability. I, for one, am no great whiz at languages, and my struggle to master, uh, communicate with field languages has been a challenge. This is complicated by the fact that field languages often differ from national languages. So, for my Iran research, I started studying Persian (*Farsi*), but when I spoke (rudimentary) Persian in Baluchistan, Shams A'din said to me, "Why do you speak to us in your language? Why don't you speak to us in ours?" And I had been so proud of speaking Persian. But I did learn Baluchi and switch over to it, which allowed me to converse with all of my informants. But I was never fluent, and it was always a struggle to understand fully. And it was very tiring to wrestle with the local language all of the time. Thus much time and energy is often devoted simply to language, which reduces the time and energy available for the research itself.

Let's not kid ourselves: to be a "real" cultural anthropologist, you have to conduct field research. That's a matter of image. But it is also true that you cannot establish new knowledge without new information, so some kind of research is required. And while it is possible to do your anthropology in libraries and archives, even original research, it is not regarded as adequate, at least not for cultural anthropologists. Fieldwork is necessary. One reason is, and this is the great thing about fieldwork, you *discover* things that you had not imagined. When I began research on the Baluchi tribe, I thought of them, as they and other Middle Eastern tribes are generally discussed in the literature, as herders or pastoralists, and they did herd goats, sheep, and camels. And they liked to characterize themselves as *wasildar*, livestock owners. But, and this is what I discovered, they really had a mixed "multiresource" economy, depending on herding; cultivation of grains and date palms; hunting and gathering; in the past, predatory raiding; and, more recently, migrant labor and transporting goods and trading. So while commentators, and the people themselves, like to stress one aspect of their activity, usually the most prestigious, the reality discovered through fieldwork is more complex and more interesting.

Biological Anthropology

Barbara J. King
College of William and Mary

"Good morning, Kuja; good morning, Mandara; good morning, Kwame . . ." I greet the gorillas at the National Zoological Park's Great Ape House one by one. Mandara, the nurturing "supermom," only shoots me a glance, but Kuja, the group's silverback leader, offers a deep rumble in reply. Kwame, the juvenile son of Mandara and Kuja, barrels right up to the cage mesh and bangs on the metal in a bid to assert his dominance. The other gorillas respond too, according to their personality and the mood of the moment.

I have enjoyed these greeting rituals for many years. For biological anthropologists like me who specialize in primate behavior, gone are the days of recording data on monkeys or apes with a neutral demeanor. Aiming for total emotional detachment, in the service of objectivity, was the norm in the 1980s when I started as a graduate student. In those days, when I observed orangutans in the zoo, or baboons in the Kenyan bush, I tried to emulate the proverbial fly on the wall; that is, being keenly watchful but as non-intrusive as possible. Times have changed. For one thing, there is a growing recognition that objectivity may neither be possible nor wholly desirable in interpreting what animals do; experts like Jane Goodall and Marc Bekoff counsel that "a feel for the organism" may become a source of real scientific insight. For another, we know so much more now about the complexity of nonhuman primates' cognitive and emotional responses to the world—including responses to the arrival of *Homo sapiens* in their midst. I feel confident that none of us would enter a friend's home without offering a polite greeting to her and to her family. Apes are not people, but they are sentient, feeling creatures, and when I walk into their home, I greet them as such.

In most years since 1997, my undergraduate students at the College of William and Mary and I have studied gestural communication in apes. The basic principles of our research framework include:

- Any ape group, like any human group, is a system. This means that an action taken or an emotion expressed by one group member may ripple throughout the group. Even when we sample the behavior of a single animal or a single pair, we remain tuned in to dynamic shifts in the group as a whole.

- Numbers don't tell the whole story. Many primatologists invest heavily in quantifying and statistically analyzing the behavior patterns they see. This approach is often valuable. For someone interested in communication, however, the *quality* of actions taken and emotions expressed is paramount, and as a result, qualitative work is key. This doesn't mean that I collect anecdotes. It means that I analyze in detail interactions filmed over many months, in order to capture the subtle features of the contingent "dynamic dance" between two or more apes. The limb and head movements made by the apes, the coordination (or lack of it) between two apes' movements, and the degree of muscular tension visible in the apes' bodies are among the things to which I attend.
- The case study approach, based on long-term observations, is valuable. To work toward contrasting the communicative patterns of one gorilla group with another is laudable, but qualitative work within a single group is also valuable. With an interest in developmental dynamics, I trace the trajectory of gestural patterns by infants as they grow into juveniles. Comparison can thus be made across gorilla youngsters and within the same youngster but across different developmental periods.

How do we actually carry out the work? On a zoo observation morning, one person on the research team:

- Films for an hour, focusing for 15 minutes at a time on one infant or juvenile, then switching to the next;
- Moves to the nonpublic area, where we can greet, observe up close, hear, and smell (but never touch) the gorillas, and take data on paper;
- Consults with zoo staff; the experienced keepers know and record the apes' daily actions, and their health histories in great detail.

Once back on campus and at home, the work continues. At that point, we watch and rewatch the films in order to take highly detailed notes, using previously worked-out definitions and descriptive measures about the interactions. Then I:

- Write up the data and publish, teach, and speak about it for both academic and popular audiences. Video clips help convey how gorillas communicate and about what we may learn from the ape data more generally such as about origins of language.
- Work with other researchers to enable the comparative perspective to gain rigor. Currently, I am co-authoring a paper with Marcus Perlman (Psychology, University of California Santa Cruz) and Joanne Tanner (Psychology, Scottish Primate Research Group) to analyze data (quantitatively and qualitatively) from filmed records on gorillas at the San Francisco Zoo.
- Remember—and teach, write, and speak about—primatologists' responsibility toward the apes, whether in captivity (www.savethechimps.org/) or the wild (www.bushmeat.org).

Some biological anthropologists research and study hominid fossils; others trace patterns of DNA in human populations, and still others endeavor to understand the adaptation of modern humans to scorching-hot deserts or stressful high altitudes. Biological anthropology fieldwork and lab work are at times exciting and at times tedious, but they always contribute to the body of anthropological scholarship about what it means to be human. For me, it is the apes that endlessly fascinate because of their smartness, their deep emotional connections to each other, and the clues they hold for helping anthropologists understand the evolved balance between ape-human continuities and discontinuities.

Archaeology

Norah Moloney

Institute of Archaeology, University College London

For the most part, archaeological excavations are summer events, scheduled to coincide with university and college vacation when staff and students are free to devote time to "doing" field archaeology. Excavations allow new students to test archaeological techniques taught in lectures and practicals during the year. Those with excavation experience may be given particular responsibilities such as supervision of excavation areas, organization of finds processing, archaeobotanical retrieval, data entry, and helping beginners. Regular, active participation in all aspects of excavation, combined with the curiosity to discover the how and why of fieldwork, are the building materials that make good field archaeologists.

Archaeological excavations don't happen at the whim of the director. Excavations have a goal, be it to check for the presence of archaeological remains prior to modern development or to investigate a research question such as lifestyles of past groups. The former comes under the domain of Cultural Resource Management (CRM), is in essence rescue work driven by a tight time schedule, and is the business of contract archaeology. Research-based excavation is usually university led, generally with more flexibility in time, but always constrained by limited finances.

The beginning of an excavation is preceded by months of planning: applying for official permits and funding; and organizing the excavation and laboratory equipment, as well as health and safety needs, housing, food, and transport. Then it is necessary to determine and justify where, what, and how to excavate. As sites vary enormously from large urban, historic settlements to small archaic campsites, so too do approaches to excavation. For example, on a small archaic campsite, every detail and find is recorded, something that is clearly impossible when excavating a large urban center.

Buendia Rockshelter: **Buendia Rockshelter** in Spain is a small site that dates to between 15,000 and 14,000 years ago, a period known as the Upper Paleolithic (or Late Stone Age). As this is a time before the development of pottery and metals, archaeological finds on Upper Paleolithic sites predominantly consist of stone tools and animal bones. Bone, antler, and shell artifacts are occasionally found at such sites and, in exceptional cases, art objects such as beads, figurines, and cave art. At Buendia, we have found thousands of stone tools, but fewer animal bones because the sediments in most levels of the site preserve bone poorly. But we have recovered fragments of bone harpoons, shells from the Mediterranean region some 200 miles away, and stones covered with ocher (a natural reddish/yellowish pigment). Our excavations have revealed "in situ" knapping floors (exact areas where people made stone tools), traces of ancient camp fires, and charcoal remains, some of which have allowed us to get radiocarbon dates for the site.

The Buendia team is a small group of about 16 people from various parts of Europe and North America. We live in a village about 5 miles from the site. Each day, part of the group works on the site, while the rest work in the site laboratory in the village. Work schedules are arranged so that everyone is able to experience all aspects of practical excavation and laboratory work to gain a comprehensive understanding of the many facets of fieldwork.

Work at the site: After a 5-mile drive through a landscape of sunflower fields and olive groves, we arrive on site in time to start work at 8 am. The first job is to remove the protective material covering the excavation floor. Then the director discusses with us the day's strategy, what we should be looking for (changes in sediment type or color, changes in finds), and assigns each person to a particular area. The excavation follows an open area technique, which means that the site isn't divided into separate squares but that we excavate the surface as one unit to reveal each archaeological level as it occurs. In this way, we see patterns of activity across the site that reflect a particular slice of time.

On Paleolithic excavations such as Buendia, the tools of the trade are very fine; we dig with screwdrivers and thin wooden skewers to ensure that we don't miss or damage material, or mix up the sediments. We also remove our shoes to avoid damaging the archaeological floor. The site is small enough that we can work from around the edges and so avoid stepping on the archaeological surface. On some Paleolithic sites excavators sit on planks that are raised slightly above the floor surface. In either case, excavating positions are rarely consistently comfortable and there usually comes a time when your body complains loudly.

We mark each find with a pin, and at regular periods these are recorded. Accurate recording is crucial to enable later computer reconstruction of the archaeological floor. We number our finds sequentially on a record sheet, noting the type of material, and find (bone, stone tool, etc.) before they are recorded electronically. At Buendia, we use a "total station" that records and stores data on the orientation of each piece, and its location on the horizontal and vertical plane that is later downloaded to a computer. Each piece is then placed in a bag with its number for transport to the lab.

All sediment removed during excavation is dry sieved to collect any tiny artifacts missed in excavation; but keeping in mind that many pieces are less than one centimeter in size, it is amazing how few pieces people miss. A comprehensive flotation sampling of sediments is undertaken for the recovery of any archaeobotanical remains.

Back in the Lab: On arrival back at the lab, the first job is to check the day's finds against recording sheets. While two people do this, another person downloads the total station data into the computer, where software converts it into diagrams of the horizontal and vertical patterns of the day's finds. Often patterns indicate a clear separation of levels, but not always; life isn't that easy. Interested students gather around the computer and try to interpret the diagrams: Are different levels indicated? Are levels mixed up? If so, is there a way of separating them?

Processing of finds in the lab follows a number of stages: washing, drying, labeling, initial classification (e.g., stone tool type), confirmation of the initial classification by a specialist, measurements of finds, and then entry into the computer of this basic data. As in the field, lab work generates a buzz of activity, discussion, and increasing interest in, and knowledge of, the materials that pass through our hands.

There is plenty of material for student projects. Refitting lithics allows the partial (or if we are especially lucky, the full) reconstruction of the stone tool manufacturing process, thus providing a window on the technological strategies and decisions made by the Stone Age inhabitants of Buendia when working stone. It is clear that they used different types of flint, and survey of the surrounding landscape has revealed a number of sources within a few kilometers of the site.

So what have we learned so far about the ancient inhabitants of Buendia? The stratigraphic levels indicate that there were repeated occupations of the rockshelter over a period of perhaps 700 years or so, at a time when much of northern Europe was covered in ice sheets and the climate in central Spain was dry and very cold. Groups made their tools, sometimes in the shelter itself, from locally collected flint. Some groups made large, blade-like tools while others preferred very small tools called microliths that they hafted, probably on wooden or bone handles. At times, they also made bone spears (probably many more than have been preserved at the site) that they could have used for hunting game, such as horse, goat, and deer (remains of which we have found). Fires were important to provide heat and light in the cold climate, and to cook food. It's easy, then, to imagine people sitting around the fire, working, chatting, cooking, and eating. These were mobile hunter-gatherer groups who may have traded or picked up Mediterranean sea shells on their travels, but we can't be sure whether these shells were for decoration or filled other purposes, although they are definitely too small to be food. There are a few enigmatic, ocher-stained stone slabs that, because they are rare finds, might indicate symbolic activity. Also intriguing is a deliberately dug pit partially exposed in a stratigraphic section, in which bones and much larger stone tools than are usual at the site have been deposited. Such a feature is most unusual in Upper Paleolithic sites in Spain, but we won't know the exact contents of the pit until the whole excavation area reaches the pit level, hopefully during the next excavation.

The Buendia excavations are beginning to reveal some interesting and exciting glimpses into human life in central Spain during the Ice Age, but much more remains to be discovered through excavation and later in-depth studies. Excavation and lab work are satisfying intellectual and practical experiences, but they are not the only experiences we gain; fieldwork is also a highly social activity generating wonderful memories of a great time in the field.

Linguistic Anthropology

Norma Mendoza-Denton

University of Arizona

One of my undergraduate students once invited me to a party hosted by her mom. She neglected to tell me that it was a political event, and that the congressman representing my district would be there. When the congressman asked, "So what does a linguistic anthropologist do?" I replied, "well, broadly speaking, we study language in society. We might study groups of people, or individual conversations. For instance, if I wanted to study this conversation you and I are having, I might place a video camera here to our left, and drop a microphone from the ceiling, and . . ." he looked attentively at me. I continued, ". . . and . . . how would you like to be involved in such a study? It's never been done in Arizona." The congressman blinked for a moment, and said, "well, I'll think about it; why don't you submit a proposal to my office after the election?"

Sometimes other anthropologists think of linguistic anthropologists as the scholars who are tracking down unknown languages, Indiana Jones-style, as in the recent independent movie, *The Linguists*. In reality, the work shown in the movie captures a limited (and somewhat controversial) part of what linguists and linguistic anthropologists do. Most of us study language as the expressive medium that shapes, constitutes, and reflects wider social patterns. Since the 1960s, linguistic anthropologists have sought to go beyond traditional grammatical descriptions of "exotic" languages to place an emphasis on the uses to which language is put. Discovering ways of speaking might involve finding out what counts as a request, what situations require a greeting, how one marks irony or politeness, and what might be the appropriate length of a pause. In short, what are culturally specific ways that language structure and language use might be organized?

In the fall, after the election, I obtained Institutional Review Board (Human Subjects) clearance and submitted a proposal to study political discourse interactions centered around the office of then Congressman Jim Kolbe, R-AZ (fifth district). In some ways, the hardest part of the project was getting funding. It was hard to convince agencies and review boards that the project was a nonpartisan investigation, and they often asked that the proposal be modified to include study of a Democrat. This was not possible for practical reasons: I wanted to start on the project during the school year since I couldn't believe my luck that the congressman had agreed, and also because the nearest Democratic congressperson at the time lived more than 2 hours away and didn't hold frequent town hall meetings. The project began with much-appreciated funding from the University of Arizona and from my department.

The fieldwork took place from 2000 to 2001, and involved me (and my then undergraduate student Ashley Stinnett, now a Ph.D. student at the University of Arizona) following Congressman Kolbe (hereafter Rep. Kolbe) to town hall meetings, Fourth of July parades, picnic cookouts, supermarket inaugurations, and protests, and on two occasions to Washington, DC. We also obtained a sampling of

Rep. Kolbe's campaign commercials and collected his speech during a sociolinguistic interview with laboratory-quality sound. In addition, we conducted some interviews with constituents who were present at the meetings.

We collected approximately 60 hours of video- and audio-taped data, and have been transcribing and analyzing them, focusing until now on what I call the irate constituent series. These are the people who came to the publicly advertised town hall meetings to air a complaint. In the airing of the complaint, sometimes they were prepared with props and literature and arguments, and sometimes they became agitated. I am broadly interested in the study of conflictive interaction, so in some ways this was the best place for me to start looking at these data.

The techniques available to linguistic anthropologists are very broad, and for this particular project they include:

- **Textual Analysis.** It is important in this study to place the politician's action within its political context, so we tracked down constituent reaction in the press, the congressional voting record, and newspaper accounts of the political setting.
- **Video Ethnography.** This was the main method of data collection for this study. At every town hall meeting and political event, my research assistant(s) and I would videotape and take fieldnotes on the live political events unfolding before us. Sometimes we were fortunate to have two cameras rolling. This became especially useful when we ventured into gesture analysis.
- **Discourse Analysis.** Detailed transcription of the speech events in conjunction with an understanding of the political backdrop allows us to carry out an investigation into the themes that crosscut the various specific instances of the interaction. For instance, how do politicians talk about the United States and other countries deploying "friendship" metaphors? How are countries that are "friends" supposed to act? Some of the data from our visit to Washington, DC, are especially rich in "friend" metaphors.
- **Conversation Analysis.** The close analysis of face-to-face interaction is an especially powerful tool to look at Rep. Kolbe's encounters with constituents. What are the patterns of turn-taking, topic control, and response allocation? What interactional moves are speakers making to allow them to gain control of the floor?
- **Quantitative Sociolinguistics.** The low-level patterning of speech (below the level of the sentence) is also an object for linguistic analysis. In my case, I am interested in the ways in which Congressman Kolbe "adjusts" his speech or accommodates to the speech style of his constituents, even in conditions of conflict. This is why it is useful to gather his speech from many different settings, from a formal interview conducted in conditions of perfect quiet, where he is uttering isolated words with no distractions, ranging through interactions with his Arizona constituents visiting him in DC, all the way to his reaction when one of the irate constituents in a town hall meeting is talking to him. Measuring and quantifying linguistic elements that may capture this accommodation is one of the tools of a quantitative sociolinguistic/ethnographer.

Integrating these multimodal tools in analysis has allowed us to advance some novel claims with regard to the alignment of gesture and intonation, and to look at a case study of the ways in which an irate constituent's gestures amplify her argument to delineate the political public sphere (for which she holds Rep. Kolbe responsible). Some of these findings are forthcoming in a paper coauthored by me with Stefanie Jannedy for the *Journal of English Linguistics*. Other research that I am still developing includes the accommodation of Rep. Kolbe to his constituents at the level of the sound system, and aspects of coordinated breathing between inter-actants at a town hall meeting.

As Philip Carl Salzman noted in his part of this fieldwork chapter, we have many tools at our disposal in our anthropological toolkits. For multimedia ethnographers, it is essential to set up the field site in such a way that video and audio recording permissions are obtained ethically from the participants. It is also essential to know one's way around the equipment. Many a crucial point has been lost due to a malfunctioning microphone or video camera, so my first advice would be to practice, practice, practice with all your equipment before you go! Get comfortable with video and audio recording, and make sure all of your equipment has the right foreign voltage adapters, and that you won't go into a house in a remote setting and knock out their electricity with your energy-hogging equipment. If you use video, I suggest that a pre-fieldwork course on digital video or ethnographic filmmaking is important to get the most out of your technology. It is impossible when working with video and audio equipment to avoid the "observer's paradox," a phenomenon that, as William Labov suggests, means that merely being present as an observer in a linguistic setting changes the speech. Therefore, there is no way to collect interview data without affecting it, but one can mitigate it by both being considerate of the participants such as not taping restricted religious ceremonies for instance, by treating the recording equipment as "no big deal," and by habituating participants to its presence.

Linguistic anthropologists can sometimes span the methods of linguistics, cultural anthropology, and occasionally other subfields such as archaeology or biology. For example, I collaborate with my colleague David Raichien, a biological anthropologist, on some of the breathing work. Before beginning fieldwork, a strong research proposal and familiarity with your equipment is essential. After coming home from the field with your data, keeping your eyes open to novel methods for understanding your data is equally important.

STUDY QUESTIONS

1. You are going to do some "mental fieldwork." Mentally decide where you want to go and what you want to study in each of the 4 anthropological subfields. For examples: Fiji Island food; black and white colobus monkey reactions to eagles in Uganda; Neolithic plates in Jordan; a comparison of 2 click language dialects in South Africa. Pick any 2 of them and write out a plan of fieldwork from beginning to end.

CHAPTER 14

How to Take Anthropology Tests

Mary Pulford

Lake Superior College

Patricia C. Rice

West Virginia University

Instructors and students agree on one thing: they hate to give and take exams. But, unfortunately, it is often the only way instructors can evaluate students; and because evaluation is a required part of your college career, it is never too early to think about testing. You probably received a syllabus for this class on the first day, so you already know which type of evaluation will be required during the term. In seminars and some upper-division courses, a lengthy term paper, usually based on library or original research, may be the only evaluation. But in introductory-level courses, you will be expected to take tests that will include one or some combination of multiple choice questions, true/false questions, short-term identifications, and essays, short or long. This chapter will help you think about tests before, during, and after; it should help you with every test in this course and perhaps in other courses as well.

Test taking is a skill that can be enhanced by learning how to take them. Some students are "test smart," which means they find taking tests to be easy and even fun, and they do well on them. Other students do not do well on tests just because they are not "test smart." Because being or not being "test smart" is not part of what instructors want to grade you on, we hope that this chapter will help to level the playing field.

But before we start making suggestions about how to take anthropology tests, you must be aware that test taking is close to the end of a progressive line; only the final grade and getting credit for the course comes after testing. We think it is important to start at the beginning of the process, to put taking tests in proper context. The first question to ask and answer is, "What is a test, and what does it purport to do?" Tests are questions that pertain to what you are expected to learn in a particular course, and taking a test entails answering those questions. We are talking about tests for a particular course, such as the anthropology course you are enrolled in. Whether the test is short or long, whether there are 3 or 4 tests during the term or just a midterm and final, whether the final exam is comprehensive or not, each will test your mastery of certain assigned materials. Normally that involves written materials (certain chapters in a textbook or assigned readings) and in-class materials (lectures, discussions, questions and answers, and exercises); it may also involve assignments done on the Internet.

Our Advice

Know what you will be tested on; check the syllabus, and if in doubt, ask your instructor. Read all of the written materials at least once when assigned, underlining or highlighting principles or what your instructor says to look for in the readings; reread either the entire assignment or your underlinings or highlightings before the test. Spend just as much time, if not more, on reviewing in-class materials. Do not miss class unless absolutely necessary. When making out a test, your instructor must assume you have been to every session. Remember that your instructor believes that what he or she presents in class is important. Most tests will cover both readings and in-class materials but may vary in how each will be weighed. Unless your instructor tells you to the contrary, assume that tests will weigh half on readings and half on class materials. If in doubt, ask your instructor.

Don't miss class, and take good notes. Most instructors will allow tape recordings of your sessions, but be sure to get informed consent prior to recording any session (See Chapter 8 on ethics). You need not write down every word your instructor says, but be sure you note all concepts, principles, and identifications, with enough detail to define them, because that is often what shows up on tests. Instructors often put key words and phrases on the chalkboard, so be sure to note them and their importance. If you must miss a class, get notes from someone who was there. If you go to class every session and study your notes, you can get every in-class question correct on the test; if you get notes from someone else who was there, you probably will get half of the in-class questions right; if you don't go to class and therefore can't study these materials, you may get 25 percent. Because most essay questions are generated from in-class materials, you will probably do very poorly on essays that were based on topics discussed in any class that you missed. Many instructors have set up online chat rooms to compliment in-class discussions. We encourage you to participate in these chat rooms or at least read through what other students are writing and thinking about. These types of discussions can expand your thinking and perceptions of issues and ideas.

MULTIPLE CHOICE QUESTIONS

Some exams are made up of only multiple choice questions; this is particularly true in large classes. Other tests are a mixed bag of some multiple choice questions and some essays, short or long. Multiple choice questions can vary from a lead statement with one correct clause to correctly complete the statement to questions that ask you to find two correct answers or decide whether all or none of the answers is correct. Some questions are negative questions with "not" or "never" in them; here you will have to decide which answers make correct statements and which one does not. Some questions are factual, and some attempt to make you think about the answer. How do you take multiple choice tests?

If you don't go to class on a steady basis, you will have to guess at the answers, and if there are four possible answers, you can expect to get only 25 percent correct on that test. The rest of this discussion is based on the assumption that you are attending class regularly; otherwise, we cannot help you.

What follows is based on the assumption that your instructor wants to find out what you know from his or her class. Try to deconstruct the making of a test by putting yourself in the shoes of an instructor. Because instructors want to know how much you have mastered of certain materials, when they sit down at their desks and contemplate making out tests, their thinking goes something like this: "How do I find out what the students know about topic X?" The answer to this question becomes a lead statement about topic X. For example, your instructor may decide he or she wants to find out whether you know about the relative distribution of Neandertal fossils and artifacts 50,000 years ago. So, a question might be:

The largest number of Neandertal fossils has been found in:
    (a) Italy.   (c) Germany.
    (b) Israel.   (d) France.

A negatively put question could be:

In all but which of the following places do we find Neandertal bones?
    (a) France.   (c) Kenya.
    (b) Israel.   (d) Iran.

Other questions can attempt to make you think through a question rather than regurgitate a memorized answer. Such a "thought question" might be:

Given the dates of fossils and artifacts of Neandertal and anatomically modern humans, the likely relationship between the two populations is:

    (a) Neandertal and modern humans never met because the dates do not overlap.
    (b) Because the dates overlap a few hundred years but only in eastern Europe, they probably did not run into each other.

(c) The dates overlap by thousands of years, and because only modern humans survived, it is likely that they killed off or outcompeted Neandertal.
(d) The dates overlap by thousands of years, and they either ignored each other or made love, not war, as there is no evidence of conflict.

After writing the lead statement, instructors must then ponder the possible answers (clauses that complete the statement). One clause is easy: the correct one. The harder ones are the incorrect ones because they must be plausible to the student who has not done his or her work and is only guessing but obviously incorrect to the student who knows the correct answer. And that's how instructors make out multiple choice questions. Knowing how they do it may help you in taking tests.

Let's assume you are a good student who has gone to class regularly, read the assigned readings, and studied for the test. Some students have no problem looking at each question with its possible answers and picking the correct one. They simply know it to be the correct answer and know that the others are incorrect. But remember that your instructor must construct answers that are not dead giveaways, and those "other 3 answers" may have bits of correctness in them. How do you handle that? Easy: don't look at the answers! Sometimes answers confuse students, although the lead statement doesn't. So if your test has the answers on a separate line from the lead statement, don't look at the answers, but mentally answer the question before looking at the choices given. Then it is usually easy to find the same answer you told yourself was correct from the answers provided. Or cover up the answers with your hand or a blank card if your eye wants to wander down to the answers, and do the same thing: tell yourself how to complete the lead statement, and then find it in the answer choices. Most multiple choice questions lend themselves to this treatment.

If you get in the habit of covering up the answers until you have mentally answered each lead statement question, you will find that you don't leave out questions, nor do you answer them too hurriedly. Don't look for recognizable words; look at the complete statement.

Finally, most multiple choice questions are answered on mechanically graded answer sheets such as Scantron sheets. Far too many students leave one or two answers blank, mark two answers, or forget to do the last page of questions.

Our Advice

Take a few minutes to go over your answers to see that you did not make any of these mistakes. Carefully erase your answers if you change your mind, and erase any notations you may have made on the sheet. The sheets are very sensitive to pencil marks and pick up graphite very easily; extraneous pencil marks may make your answers appear incorrect. Mechanically graded answer sheets are meant to save the instructor's time, so you cannot expect him or her to go over each test individually to make sure every question is answered or that there are no extraneous marks on the sheet. Don't lose points this way.

TRUE/FALSE QUESTIONS

True/false questions usually hinge on one or two words. Look for words such as "always," "never," and "seldom," because often the statement you have to judge as correct or incorrect hinges on whether the adverbial phrase is correct. (Multiple choice questions often use the same adverbs.) A statement such as "All humans have 23 chromosomes" is incorrect for two reasons: some humans have an extra chromosome, and humans have 23 *pairs* of chromosomes. If the statement said, "Most humans have 23 pairs of chromosomes," it would be correct. Remember that "all" means 100 percent, "most" means more than half, "some" means less than half, "a few" means less than 10 percent, and "none" means 0.

True/false questions often put two possibly linked items together and ask you whether they are linked. Sometimes, the linkage is between a place and a happening, as in "The Trojan Wars took place in Greece." If the linkage between the happening and the place is incorrect, then obviously the statement is false. If three things are linked, as in "The Trojan War took place in Greece in the third century A.D.," and either the time or place is incorrect, the statement is false. Sometimes the linkage is between the past and the present, as in "The Anasazi made kivas, but their modern descendants, the Hopi, do not." Sometimes the linkage is between two or more parts of some phenomenon, such as "Pottery and farming are always associated with sedentary life." But note that in each of these linkages, there is also a real or implied adverb such as "always" or "never." They are the words to look for.

DEFINITIONS AND SHORT IDENTIFICATIONS

Often anthropological concepts and terms are so important that they must be internalized or memorized, and your instructor may ask you to identify some of them to make sure you have mastered them. You should highlight or underline all such important words in your in-class notes (and know the definitions) and use the glossary that normally is at the end of chapters in texts. That's usually where your instructor will get the words to ask you about in the first place. When you write them out, be clear and brief, but convey the gist of the term or concept. If you can say it slightly differently from your instructor or the text and yet keep its precise meaning, this tells your instructor that you really understand the term.

ESSAY QUESTIONS

Essay tests often are designed to test a student's overall knowledge, depth of comprehension of an issue or concept, and critical thinking skills. Even if you haven't taken freshman composition yet or your writing skills are not quite what they should be, you can still do well on essay tests.

Our Advice

Preparing for essay tests takes the same path as preparing for multiple choice tests: go to class, read all of the assignments, and take good notes. If the syllabus clearly states that essay tests will be the standard form, ask the instructor for a sample question or two. You might also consider asking the instructor what criteria he or she will use to assess your essay. And what is the format for taking the essays? Will the instructor hand out sheets of paper with the questions and then a space to write, or will you be using a composition book? If you are required to answer the questions in a composition book, then you will probably be writing significantly longer and more complex essays.

Essay tests are designed to test your ability to explain in detail and in depth a particular issue or question. In cultural anthropology you might get an essay question like this: "Define the concept of enculturation and explain how this concept applies to the general notion of culture." You should start by defining in some detail the concept of enculturation, explain how it works, and discuss its impact on the individual; then give some examples from your own life and from readings or films. Then describe how enculturation affects the lives of individual adults and a group or society. You might end by comparing the enculturation of children in your own culture with that of another. Is the process the same, or are the outcomes different?

Now you know how to think about answering an essay question in the area of cultural anthropology, but what about archaeology or physical anthropology? Aren't those two areas of anthropology only about facts? Hardly; read on.

Let's suppose you get the following question: "Define and discuss the implications of bipedal locomotion." To start, you need to define what it means to be a bipedal hominid. Remember that birds are bipedal, too! You need to discuss how bipedalism works in hominid survival. What are the benefits to being bipedal? Does being bipedal contribute to social organization in any way? What are the disadvantages of being a bipedal hominid? Do the advantages outweigh the disadvantages?

Our Advice

One of the best ways to take an essay test is not to write what you are thinking but to think about what you want to write. Prepare a written outline. Ask yourself, "What do I want to write? Do my sentences and paragraphs flow together to show that I really do understand the concept? Do my ideas flow together? How will I make my argument or build my case to answer the question?"

You might practice writing an essay answer. And then ask someone to read and critique it and reciprocate when that person needs the same kind of help.

One problem many students have who don't pre-think or outline their essay answers is that when they start to write, they write everything they know about an issue or question in one long paragraph. Fifty factual sentences strung together in one long paragraph isn't what your instructor wants to read. Can you connect those facts? Can you explain the big picture? What are the implications of all of those facts?

Write clearly. Good handwriting or printing is a must here. If your instructor cannot read your handwriting, no matter how great the content is, your grade might suffer. Use a good pencil or black or blue ink. Always have a good eraser that you know works! Take your time reading and answering the test. If you have an hour to do the test, use the entire hour if needed. Try to get to the classroom 10 minutes before the test starts, to get settled, clear your mind, and prepare yourself mentally.

Finally, read over your essays. If you don't reread them, you can't correct them. It is worth the extra minute or two to reread your answers.

AFTER THE EXAM

What if you didn't do well on your first test, regardless of whether it was multiple choice or essay? You should look carefully over your test to see where there is room for improvement. Did the instructor make notes on your essays that would be helpful for the next test? Did you misplace a mark on the Scantron sheets? Were you properly prepared? A visit to your instructor during his or her office hours might help you improve your next test score. And you might consider a group study session for the next test. Some students do better studying alone, and some do better studying with other students preparing for the same exam. If your study habits for the first exam paid off with a good grade, stick with them. In the long run, you are the only one who knows what's best for you. If the results of that first exam were not to your liking, consider changing to another method.

Finally, don't let one bad grade turn you off in a course. Most instructors consider grade improvement in a positive light and are very willing to help you improve your scores. Sometimes a certain kind of testing does not indicate how much you know; if this is true for you, feel free to discuss this with your instructor because there may be another way to test what you do know. Don't wait until the day before the last exam and then tell your instructor that you're having trouble. Improvement starts with the second exam.

Glossary

Accountability: The ethical principle concerning whether anthropologists owe their allegiance to the people being studied or to the group funding the research.

Adaptation: The theoretical end result of natural selection on biological species; species are generally better adapted to their existing environment through time.

Agriculture: Technically, domestication of plants using plows or draft animals, but often used interchangeably with "cultivation," "horticulture," and farming.

Applied anthropology: The subfield that attempts to use knowledge gained by original research to help solve human problems in any or all other subfields.

Archaeology: The subfield that focuses on the study and explanation of our human cultural past.

Artifacts: Material remains of past cultures in the form of tools, features (postholes, footprints), shelter, and so on.

Bioanthropology: The subfield that focuses on the study and analysis of our biological past and present; sometimes called physical anthropology.

Biological change: Same as "evolution," the change of a population from its ancestral state to a more modern state.

Cave paintings: Upper Paleolithic portrayals of mostly animals that were hunted and eaten between 40,000 and 10,000 years ago in Europe.

Contingent groups: Groups that are formed "as needed," such as during times of warfare.

Cultivation: Technically, taking care of wild plants by guarding, weeding, watering, and so on but often used synonymously with farming.

Cultural anthropology: The subfield that focuses on the culture of modern people.

Cultural ecology (or ecoculturalism): A theoretical perspective that focuses on the interrelationships between cultures and their environment, sometimes as a possible causation of change.

Cultural relativism: A basic principle of cultural anthropology that says that anthropologists must suspend their personal ideas of right and wrong and look only at other cultures relative to their own standards.

Culture: "A way of life"; the different sets of behaviors, cognition, and emotions that characterize the learned, shared, and integrated portion of what it is to be human.

Culture change: The process that all cultures go through in time; opposite of stasis.

Darwinian gradualism: The belief that, in general, species evolve slowly and continuously through time with few, if any, large changes in short periods of time.

Data: Same as "evidence"; facts or research findings that support or falsify hypotheses.

Deductive approach: One of two approaches to the scientific method where a hypothesis is generated before any data are collected to test the hypothesis for its support or falsification.

Development: The use of basic and applied research to develop specific programs to solve specific human problems.

Diffusionism: A theoretical approach that focuses on the borrowing (diffusion) of cultural traits from one group to another.

Domestication: The process of changing wild plants and animals into genetically different plants and animals; the process involves purposeful selection of desired traits.

DNA: The physical basis of heredity carried in cell nuclei.

Drift: One cause of evolutionary change where small populations, usually isolated, change their gene frequencies from one generation to the next just because of the effect of small numbers.

Emic approach: Insider's (or "native") perspective of how individual cultures operate.

Empiricism: Technically, refers to obtaining data by using the human senses, particularly that of vision; also an early paradigm that assumed scientists were unbiased and totally objective.

Ethical relativism: Technically, the suspension by anthropologists (and others) of all judgment on any and all cultural practices of all cultures and groups.

Ethnography: The cultural study of a single cultural group and often the written description of that particular culture.

Etic approach: An outsider's perspective; usually in cross-cultural perspective.

Eugenics: A movement in the United States and other countries whose main aim was to "better" the genetics of the human species by restricting the number of offspring in those groups the movement regarded as "inferior."

Evidence: Same as "data"; facts or research findings used to support or falsify a hypothesis.

Evolution: Darwin defined it as "descent with modification"; a more modern definition might claim it is the process by which one group/species of plant or animal changes over time to become a different/new population.

Explication: Those theoretically oriented explorations of meaning in some depth or elaboration rather than scientific explanations of particular phenomena.

Fieldwork: Literally, going out where the work is: biological anthropologists excavate human fossils, archaeologists excavate artifacts, cultural anthropologists go to live with modern people to study their modern culture, and linguistic anthropologists study modern languages.

Functionalism: The theoretical school that focuses on the interrelations of a culture's behaviors, cognition, and emotions to each other to ascertain how that culture "works"; often coupled with "structuralism."

Gene flow: One of the causes of evolutionary change where a population through interbreeding with individuals on its geographic borders that normally do not interbreed now exchange genes; the genes can be said to "flow" from one group to another within a species.

Handaxe: A tool of flint or other homogeneous material that is shaped by direct percussion of a hammer stone onto the flint to make a bilaterally symmetrical tool; can be 6 to 8 inches long.

Heuristic theories: The general ideas that guide inquiries in cultural anthropology such as functionalism.

Historical particularism: A theoretical approach that focuses on the diffusion or borrowing of cultural traits from one group to another.

Holism: The principle in anthropology that claims we must study the interrelationships among all facets of humanity in order to properly study humans.

Homo sapiens: Technical name of the species of modern humans.

Human Genome Project: Started in the early 1990s and all but completed in 2005; the string of 3.5 billion base pairs can now be compared among different people and also compared to different species.

Human rights: The rights of humans (dead or alive) to agree or not with the use of their bodies or opinions; the United Nations has a declaration of these rights for all people.

Human variability: Although the human species is variable in many morphological traits, until the mid-1980s, the term was used synonymously with "biological race." Now biological anthropologists conclude that the traits used to separate groups do not co-vary.

Hypothesis: A "good guess" about something worth explaining; data are gathered to support or falsify the idea. It also has the lowest level of confidence given to findings.

Ideal vs. real culture: Ideal culture is what people believe is proper and often what they tell the visiting anthropologist; real culture is what happens or is believed in reality.

Inductive approach: One of two approaches in science where data about a particular subject are freely collected with no preconceived ideas but the data then generates a hypothesis.

Informants: Individuals from cultures being investigated who give information to the anthropologist; a key informant is particularly useful.

Institutional racism: The form of racism that remains because it is sustained by laws, policies, and group practices.

Intellectual tradition: Refers to the particular paradigm that was emphasized when individuals are educated; in Western society, Old World and New World traditions exist, while in Japan, the Japanese tradition is adhered to.

Intelligence: The ability to solve problems relative to one's species (dogs solve dog problems though some do it better than others) and technologically educated humans solve technological problems better than other humans.

IQ tests and scores: The ability to answer questions posed by middle-class educators and the results of those tests.

Japanese tradition: A scientific intellectual tradition, different from the one in the West, that focuses on individual differences among monkeys for example.

Knowledge: That which is probably correct, given the nature of evidence at any one time.

Language: As opposed to speech, language is the symbolic form of communication used by many species of animals, including humans.

Law: Although it can still be falsified, a law is a theory that has been tested and retested by many scientists over many years and not falsified; it has the highest confidence level given to findings.

Lineage: The usually local level of a tribe, the members of which trace descent to the same (usually living) common ancestor.

Linguistics: The subfield that focuses on language/speech, its commonalities and differences, and its relationships to the cultures in which they are found.

Logical positivism: The current philosophy of science that assumes that scientists always have some biases but attempt to be as objective as possible in their work.

Middle-range theory: The method of science that tries to explain phenomena that are not tied to a specific time or place; more general than specific hypotheses.

Mutation: The raw material of evolutionary change where some change at the base pair level of DNA does not replicate itself identically to the parent DNA when undergoing replication.

NAGPRA: Literally, the Native American Graves Protection Repatriation Act of 1990 that specifically made it the law in the United States to offer to return Native American bones to appropriate living tribes.

Native Americans: Same as "American Indians," the inhabitants past and present of people native to the Americas.

Natural selection: One of the causes of evolutionary change based on the fact that members of any species differ in their reproductive rate and therefore have differential contributions to the next generation.

Neandertal: A population of archaic *Homo sapiens* that lived in Europe and the Middle East about 150,000 to 30,000 years ago; controversy exists about whether they interbred with immigrating modern humans, but they did become extinct while moderns survived.

Nomadism: Refers to patterns of non-sedentism where people have no permanent settlements; often associated with pastoralism or hunter–gatherers.

Nomothetic: Literally, "law like," as in finding explanations for general rather than specific knowledge.

Normative pattern: An ideal rule that is also adhered to.

Paleoanthropology: Combines the two subfields of archaeology and bioanthropology to study our human past both biologically and culturally, often emphasizing the interrelationships.

Paradigm: A philosophical/scientific way to observe a particular subject; a "lens" through which scientists see the world.

Participant observation: A research tool of cultural anthropologists who participate in the culture they are observing.

Pastoralism: A basic economy that is exclusive to herding animals; usually coupled with nomadism.

Patrilineal: Tracing descent through males only usually to establish kin groups such as patrilineages or patriclans.

Patrilocal: A rule that a married pair lives with or near the groom's family.

Pattern: Repeated behaviors or customs over time and space; sometimes called "a norm."

Peer review: The normal process of reporting research findings by using experts in the field of the research to pass judgment on the process of the research before publication.

Personal racism: As opposed to "institutional racism," the bias that individuals hold about groups of humans.

Preferential patterns: Patterns of behavior based on rules that a culture prefers, but they are not obligatory.

Proof: A word/concept never used in science because by definition scientific findings are always provisional while the word "proof" is definitive and certain.

Punctuated equilibrium: The belief that, in general, species evolve in large-scale jumps with large changes and then long periods of no change (stasis) between them.

"Race": Not a biologically valid concept; is only valid for cultural groups, and the term is close to "ethnicity."

Repatriation: The offer to turn over the bone remains of any and all Native Americans in museums and collections, or found in the future to appropriate Native American tribes under NAGPRA rules.

Scale of Change: Scale asks for the parameters of change in terms of people (one or 100 groups), time (present only for the last 1,000 years), etc.

Scientific Method: The method of doing science starting with something worth investigating followed by either inductive or deductive methods, data collection/evidence, testing the hypothesis, and reaching conclusions. All conclusions are provisional.

Sedentism: Staying in one place more or less permanently rather than migrating periodically.

Sickle cell anemia: A blood condition that results in the inability of oxygen to be delivered to the body's tissues, and caused by having two sickle cell genes. Usually results in death.

Sociocultural: The subfield that focuses on modern cultures as observed in the field by looking for patterns of beliefs and values and specific behaviors.

Social evolution: An early cultural approach to change that incorrectly assumed that cultures "evolved" in a rather automatic fashion from "savagery" to "barbarism" to "civilization."

Sociocultural anthropology: Same as "cultural anthropology" but with an emphasis on the social aspects of culture, its beliefs, its values, and resulting behaviors.

Specialized economy: Specialization (hunting–gathering, pastoralism, fishing, farming) as opposed to generalization occurs when a group spends most or all of its time in one basic economy.

Speciation: The process of forming new species either by a group changing and becoming so different as to necessitate a new designation or by some kind of isolation, splitting into two or more species.

Splitting/lumping: A basic philosophy in bioanthropology that depends on how much difference/similarity a specialist sees in fossil material, with splitters seeing more differences and lumpers seeing more similarities.

Subsistence economy: Technically, a society that produces and consumes everything it uses. Often used to refer to small-scale economy with a minimum of trade.

Substantive theories: Those theories that specify that a specific relationship exists between two cultural phenomena.

Testing: A part of the scientific method process: after a hypothesis is generated and data collected, the data are used to determine if the hypothesis is supported or falsified.

Theory: Generalizations rather than specific "low level" facts about some phenomena; medium level of confidence of scientific findings.

"A" theory: A specific paradigm to approach a subject, i.e., functionalism.

Truth: This is not a word used in science because it connotes absolute certainty.

Venus statuettes: A collection of about 200 small figurines of females sculpted during the Upper Paleolithic period in Europe between 30 and 10,000 years ago and related to "women" rather than "mothers."

Visual ethics: The ethical principle that all persons being filmed actually give consent to be filmed and for the film to be viewed by others.

Whistle-blowing: The act of reporting ethical or legal violations even if it might mean losing one's job.

Name Index

Subject Index

A

Adaptation, 48
Adaptive responses, 49
Adolescence, 42
Affirmative Action, 100
African Americans, 99–100
Agriculture, 9–10
AIDS, 22
Air-conditioning, 78
Altamira cave, 40
American Anthropological Association, 69–72
Androcentricity, 107
Anthropological archaeologists, 9
Applied research, 77
Applying anthropology, 77
Archaeology
    androcentrism and, 107
    artifacts and, 42–43
    fieldwork, 122–125
    holism and, 17–19
    patterns and, 6, 9
    scientific method and, 36–37
    theories and, 31–32
Artifacts, 19, 32, 42–43
Associational patterns, 8, 14

B

Baluchi nomads, 6–10, 12–13, 87, 117–120
Basic research, 77
Basseri nomads, 7–9
Behavioral patterns, 11, 14
Bias, 57–58, 60–65, 107
Biological anthropology
    androcentrism and, 107, 114
    fieldwork and, 120–122
    holism and, 19, 21–22
    patterns and, 6, 11

    scientific method and, 36, 42
    theories and, 31–33
Birth rates, 16–17
Bolivian farming methods, 78
Buendia Rockshelter, 122–125

C

Case studies, 118
Categories, 81
Central Intelligence Agency, 71
Central tendency, 7–8, 13
Change
    biological, 48–49
    continuity/discontinuity and, 59–60,
        62–64
    cultural, 49–51, 53–54
    cultural relativism and, 52–53
    early approaches to, 47–48
    in populations, 52
    scale and, 46, 51–52
Chinese birth rates, 16–17
Civil Rights Act, 100
Clinal distribution, 97
Code of Ethics (American Anthropological
    Association), 69–72
Collective responsibility, 11
Communication systems, 21, 120–121
Community patterns, 10–12
Compensation, 72
Conflicts in accountability, 71
Consent, 69–70, 74
Contingent groups, 12–13
Continuity, 60, 62–64
Conversation analysis, 126
Counting, 81, 118
Credit for research, 72
Crime prevention, 81–82

Integrated systems, 16
Integrative biocultural studies of race,
    100–102
Intellectual traditions, 58–60
Interpretationalism, 31
The Interpretation of Cultures
    (Geertz), 31
Interpretive anthropologists, 33
Interrelationships, 16–17
Intersubjective agreement, 73
Interviews, 70, 117–119
Irrigation agriculture, 9–10
Issues *vs.* problems, 80

J

Japanese society, 20
Jim Crow laws, 100

L

Land use patterns, 9
Language, 19–21, 119, 125–127
Law in scientific method, 41
Level of abstraction, 26
Level of confidence, 41
Linguistic anthropology, 6, 19–21, 37, 73,
    125–127
Logical positivists, 58
Lumping populations, 63

M

Malaria, 23
Mandatory normative patterns, 11, 14
Marriage patterns, 10–12
Mayans, 40
Meta-patterns, 12–13
Middle-range theories, 29–31, 32
Migration patterns, 7
Montserrat, 98–99
Mothering work, 108
Multiple choice questions, 130–131
Mundurucu culture, 61–62
Mutation, 48

N

NAGPRA (U.S. Native American Graves
    Protection and Repatriation Act
    of 1990), 69, 73
National Zoological Park, 120
Native Americans, 17, 59, 61, 73

Natural selection, 96–97
Neandertals, 19, 41–42, 63–64
Neolithic period, 87–89
New World tradition, 59, 62–64
Nomads, 6–10, 12–13, 86–87, 117–120
Nomothetic facts, 26
Normative patterns, 10, 14
Nuer nomads, 8–9

O

Objectivity, 73–74
Observing behaviors, 17, 119
Old World tradition, 58–59, 62–64
On the Origin of Species (Darwin), 41, 96

P

Paleoanthropology, 31–33, 62–65
Papua New Guinea, 81, 107, 109–110
Paradigms, 60–65
Participant observation, 51, 118
Patrilineal hunting bands, 29–30
Patterns
    associational, 8, 14
    behavioral, 11, 14
    contingent, 12–13
    defined, 7
    descriptive, 7–8, 10, 13, 26
    distributional, 8, 13
    economic, 7–10
    genetic, 11–12
    historical, 10, 13
    ideographic, 26
    of land use, 9
    mandatory normative, 11, 14
    marriage, family, community, 10–12
    meta-patterns, 12–13
    of migration, 7
    normative, 10, 14
    politics, 12–13
    preferential normative, 10–11, 14
    of social control, 11, 12–13
    statistical, 10–11, 14
Peer review, 73
Photographs, 74
Physical anthropologists, 6
Political patterns, 12–13
Population genetics, 97
Postmodernism, 31–32
Potsherds, 18
Preferential normative patterns, 10, 14
Primate behavior, 120–122